LIVING ON
THE WAVES

365 Daily Devotions

God Bless!
AmB

LIVING ON
THE WAVES

365 Daily Devotions

Stepping Out of the Boat
and Into Faith

Ammie Bouwman

credo
house publishers

Living on the Waves: Stepping Out of the Boat and Into Faith
Copyright © 2018 by Ammie Bouwman
All rights reserved.

Published in the United States by Credo House Publishers,
a division of Credo Communications, LLC, Grand Rapids, Michigan
credohousepublishers.com

Unless otherwise noted, Scripture quotations are from the Holy Bible,
New International Version®, NIV® Copyright ©1973, 1978, 1984, 2011
by Biblica, Inc.®. Used by permission. All rights reserved worldwide.

ISBN: 978-1-625861-20-7

Cover and interior design by Frank Gutbrod
Editing by Donna Huisjen
Cover image by Shutterstock
Interior graphic by Noun Project

Printed in the United States of America

First edition

To Leona, my grandmother.

*Thank you for the prayers you sent to heaven
and continue to pray now that you're there.
I love you and cannot wait until I see you again.*

*"You rule over the surging sea; when its waves
mount up, you still them."*

—PSALM 89:9

Contents

Introduction

A t the top of the Makhtesh Ramon in the Negev Desert, I heard God tell me it was time: time not only to tell my story to the world but to be obedient to anything He would ask me to do. In 2016 I wrote down my story *In Over My Head* and started a ministry called For His Glory, designed as a daily devotional on social media to meet people right where they were at in their walk with God and to show them how to have a closer relationship with Him. As I write this now, God has blessed For His Glory with over 330,000 followers and the promise of more to come. This book is the next step in the journey, and one I pray will be a blessing to all who read it.

Inside this book you will learn not only how to let go and find your promised land but how to be your authentic self and say your Hallelujahs in the hard times. You will spend each month focusing on a specific topic, and when you're done be able to look back and see how far you've come. Besides the daily devotional, there is a place for you to journal your prayers to God for the day and write out what God is showing you to work on. Each month is bathed with Scripture, a powerful way to experience God in your daily life and have a closer relationship with Him.

While doing this devotional will take you only a few minutes a day, it will grow your relationship with the Lord and filter down into all areas of your life. I am praying for you as you start this new journey that you will allow the Lord to invade every area of your life and be open to everything He shows you. The key is to surrender and open wide the doors that you have had shut for so long. The truth is that He already knows everything about you. Use this time to learn more about Him and about yourself.

Trust me when I say that I've had to learn to trust and return to Jesus each time I drifted away and to remember with every fiber in my being that I am His. I've stepped out into the waters of life and realized that I would rather be like Peter and be out of the boat walking toward Jesus than safe on the shore. Even if that means I will live on the waves and at times be in over my head . . .

Praying for you,
Ammie Bouwman

January

COUNT IT ALL JOY

"Blessed is the one who perseveres under trial because,
having stood the test, that person will receive
the crown of life that the Lord has promised
to those who love him."

–JAMES 1:12

The Journey Begins . . . the First Step

The first step is probably the hardest. Into the unknown, hands forward, feeling as you go, you take a step. You're not sure how it's going to feel or where the path will take you, but you've begun. On March 22, 2013, I took my first step. I walked into a house for an eight-hour day of prayer and healing, looking like I was traveling for a yearlong trip—and walked out carrying just my purse. The baggage I laid down that day was accumulated over a lifetime of hurts and lies. I had tried before to lay it down, only to pick it back up again and switch arms to carry the load differently this time. But no matter how hard I tried, I couldn't do it on my own. And neither can you. I needed Jesus to look deep into every pain, hurt, sin, and dark corner where I had hid the lies I believed about myself and expose them to His light. When He was done and I had seen the truth about the life I was living and the lies I was believing, He washed me clean, and the floodwaters of love, forgiveness, and truth came rushing in.

It doesn't matter what you're struggling with—mental illness, drugs, alcohol, pornography, eating disorder—you're medicating the symptom of a deeper issue, a deeper pain. Take the first step forward and kneel. Cry out to the Creator of the universe and ask Him to show you the truth in your own life, to heal you and wash you clean.

You've already stepped out by purchasing this book and reading the first page. I invite you on this journey of faith to keep moving forward, keep reaching out for God, keep taking a step every day. At the bottom of this page and every page, there is a place for you to journal your prayers and fears, admit your weaknesses, state your victories, and pray to Jesus, who gives us our identity and hope! I will also be with you in this journey. I'm praying for you as you begin . . .

Dear Jesus,

I ask for strength as we begin: strength to surrender before You, strength to allow You to do a great work in me; strength to face the areas in my life that need Your light. Help me, Lord, to . . .

Walk and Have Courage

So how do you keep taking a step forward, not knowing what will come? Faith. Faith in the truth that God loves you. Faith and belief in His promises. He doesn't promise it will be an easy journey, but He does promise to be with us. Start praying His Word into your life and claim His promises for yourself. Below are two passages that will help . . .

"So do not fear, for I am with you;
   do not be dismayed, for I am your God.
I will strengthen you and help you;
   I will uphold you with my righteous right hand. . . .
For I am the Lord your God
   who takes hold of your right hand
and says to you, Do not fear;
   I will help you."
—ISAIAH 41:10, 13

"How abundant are the good things
   that you have stored up for those who fear you,
that you bestow in the sight of all,
   on those who take refuge in you."
—PSALM 31:19

Dear Jesus,
Thank you for walking with me. Help me to have faith and trust You.
Help me to . . .

First Things First

Y ou need to know I'm not perfect. I don't have it all together. I make mistakes. But what I've learned is that the enemy (Satan) has come to steal and destroy, and one way he does this is through the lies he whispers to us and the lies we hear from other people. There are so many lies I believed: "You're not special." "You're not good enough." "No one will love you." "You will never get better." "You're a terrible mother." "Just drink this and you'll feel better." "You have no hope." "Where is God now?" Day after day I believed the lies, and this shaped who I was. I became less like the child God created me to be and more like a stranger standing in front of a large mirror. The reflection was full of pain, emptiness, and lack of self-esteem.

But I have good news! From this day forward you no longer have to believe the lies. Rebuke the enemy and tell him you are done listening. Ask God to fill you with truth, wisdom, and discernment. Open His Word and find the truth. It's not going to happen overnight. You will have to keep rebuking and work at not believing the lies until you know the truth. The truth is that you were created in God's image. The truth is that you're amazing! The truth is that you are loved by a heavenly Father who sent His Son to die on the cross to restore this fallen world and bridge the gap between God and us and to save us from our sin. You have hope and a future. Believe! Amen.

Dear Jesus,

Help me to listen to Your truth. I want to rebuke the enemy, but I feel weak and I've listened to his lies for so long. Help me to . . .

The Fence

It is easy to be sucked into this world. Media paints a picture of something, whatever they are selling that day, and leaves room for you to insert yourself into that picture. You can see yourself driving that new car, having luxurious skin and hair, eating at that restaurant, taking a certain diet pill, and feeling good about yourself when shopping at that certain clothing store. But sometimes we don't realize until it's too late that it was an illusion. We thought we were buying a way of life, we thought we would get this incredible feeling, but in actuality we are left empty and unfulfilled. Walking in this world is a challenging thing, especially when we are on the fence. We need to decide where we are going to walk and what we are going to believe in. Until you make that decision, you could move in and out of this world, allured by the illusion, and then, when left empty, clinging to God and asking Him for help. I've walked the fence and I'm tired of the lies. Even though the truth is sometimes hard to accept, it is consistent and God is faithful. I choose to stay off the fence. I choose to walk with God. Where are you walking today?

Dear Jesus,
Help me today to know Your truth. I know I've walked this fence and have believed the lies of this world. I want to walk with You. Help me to . . .

I'm Fine

The word *fine* was in my vocabulary for years. I could never let anyone know that I was struggling, because then I would lose control. If I could just keep my head above water, letting everyone think I had it all together, I would eventually be "fine," and no one would be the wiser. But the reality is that we all have struggles. We all have pain. We all live in the fractured world. None of us is untouched by this life. When I stopped pretending, I was able to allow someone to come alongside me and pray for me; I was able to share and talk openly and glean new ways to work through my problems. But more importantly, I was vulnerable and open to let God in and work on me from the inside out.

I challenge you today to take courage and be vulnerable. If not to anyone else, admit to God that you need Him. You will be amazed at what He does!

Dear Jesus,

Thank you for loving me. Help me to be vulnerable and open to everything You want to do in me and through me. I admit to You that I'm not fine. I'm struggling and I need . . .

Green Grass

I love green, freshly mowed grass. I love the lines in the yard and how everything looks perfect. Back in my old life, I wanted to have the greenest grass in our neighborhood. It was important for people to drive by and think, "Wow, they must have it all together in there." So I paid a lawn service to come and spray our lawn, fertilize, and maintain. And I would be out there, twice a week sometimes, mowing my incredibly green grass. But at the end of the day it didn't change anything on the inside of our home. It didn't change the fact that I struggled with mental illness, my marriage was in trouble, or that I wasn't happy. It was exhausting keeping up the illusion that everything was perfect.

Do you have something in your life that you're hiding behind? If so, it's keeping you from true community with God and with the people around you. Control is an illusion, and when we think we have control over something in our life, it's a lie from the enemy. I hid behind my neatly manicured lawn, and in the end it didn't solve my problems or fix my family. In the end all I had was green grass.

Start today, and look deep into your life to see if there is something you're doing for the sake of appearances. Ask Jesus to change your heart and way of thinking.

"Whoever conceals their sins does not prosper;
   but the one who confesses and renounces them finds mercy."
—PROVERBS 28:13

Dear Jesus,
I have been hiding. I have tried to control areas in my life and keep up appearances to my friends. I'm tired. Please change my heart. Help me today to . . .

The Small Stuff

I woke up yesterday anticipating a very busy day. Getting ready for work didn't go exactly as I had planned, and it seemed I was already starting off a bit behind schedule. I had so much to do, I had no idea how I was going to do it all. I hurriedly arrived at work and punched in four minutes late. But an hour in, a coworker asked if he could help me. He found a couple of things I needed and helped me with one small project. It was one of the things that had been weighing on me, and now it was done. I thanked him for blessing me, and as he walked away I smiled and said, "Thank you, Lord. I'm sorry I didn't hand that over to You." The rest of the day was challenging at times, but the Lord kept giving me the strength I needed. One by one things fell off my list. When I set off for the last big task, I had to deliver signs to three different locations around town. My route turned into one big circle with no backtracking, and before I knew it I was on my way home. After stopping to pick up a few groceries, I made it home before I usually do. I laughed. "Lord, You are amazing! I had more to do and I got it done in less time, and now I'm home. Thank you for a great day!"

I don't know about you, but sometimes I forget to give God my small stuff. I can remember to pray for people and our country, financial worries and health concerns. But I sometimes forget that He is just as concerned about all those things, as well as walking with me throughout my day. Our daily to-do list is sometimes our biggest battle. Don't forget to give that to God. He wants to carry not only our big stuff, but our small stuff too.

Dear Jesus,
Thank you for walking with me. Help me today to carry my small stuff, such as . . .

Less of Me . . . More of You

I was once filled with arrogance. I spent money I didn't have and lived in a glass house for everyone to see. I "needed" name brands and for people to believe I had it all together. I lived a lie, creating a perfect persona and almost believing it to be true. Almost. But when I was alone, surrounded by all my things, I was unhappy. I lived with an emptiness I couldn't fill, no matter how much I spent or how many people believed the lie. It wasn't until I gave up myself that I truly found myself in God. He emptied me of all the things that were me and filled me with Him. As I continue on this journey of life, I must continue to decrease and to allow Him to increase.

Let this be your prayer today:

Lord Jesus,
Empty me of all the things that are of me and fill me with You. Fill me with Your wisdom, so I can discern between what is of this world and what You have for me. Help me to decrease so You may increase. I love you, Lord. Amen.

Dear Jesus,
Thank you for filling me with You. Help me to . . .

What Road Are You Walking?

What road are you walking today? If the road is rich with life and happiness, praise God! But if you are walking in the desert, feeling as though everything is drying up around you, . . . praise God and do not lose faith.

Second Corinthians 4:8–9, 16–18 says this: "We are hard pressed on every side, but not crushed, perplexed, but not in despair; persecuted, but not abandoned; struck down, but not destroyed. . . . Therefore we do not lose heart. Though outwardly we are wasting away, yet inwardly we are being renewed day by day. For our light and momentary troubles are achieving for us an eternal glory that far outweights them all. So we fix our eyes not on what is seen, but on what is unseen, since what is seen is temporary, but what is unseen is eternal."

He told us this life would not be easy, but He promised to walk with us and not to forsake us. Trust His words, no matter what road you are on, and know that you are not alone.

Lord Jesus,
Thank you for this road I'm on. Even though I don't know where I'm going,
I know where I've been and I know You've walked with me. Help me to be
faithful and to trust You, even when the journey ahead seems challenging
and hard. Help me to stay on the road even when the clouds are rolling in
and it grows dark. Guard me with Your angels and protect me from evil.
Thank you for loving me and holding my hand. It is in Your precious name I
ask these things. Amen.

Dear Jesus,
Thank you for walking with me. This road I'm on right now is challenging
and I can't see what's ahead. Help me to have courage and praise You
along the way. Help me to . . .

Comfortable Shoes

I love comfortable shoes. I love getting comfortable after a nine-hour day when all I want to do is put my feet up and relax. I also love comfortable situations, in my own backyard when I know everyone and everyone knows me and I can be myself. But I have to be careful. Sometimes I say no to things because I might get uncomfortable. What if there will be a large crowd and people I don't know? Maybe they'll ask me questions to get to know me and I'll have to bring up something from my past. What about a mission trip? It's so far away, maybe it's not safe. Maybe it would just be better if I stayed home.

It's one thing to love getting comfortable, but it's another to stay comfortable because of fear of the unknown. Joshua 1:9 says "Have I not commanded you? Be strong and courageous. Do not be afraid; do not be discouraged, for the LORD your God will be with you wherever you go."

We don't have to be afraid. If we have faith that God is walking with us, even in our uncomfortable situations, He will give us the strength we need no matter where we are. Don't listen to the lies of the enemy telling you to stay home. Be obedient and follow wherever the road takes you.

Dear Jesus,
Pleaes forgive me for being too comfortable. Please give me courage and
help me today to . . .

Forest Fires

Have you ever said something, and once the words left your lips you could see the pain they caused? You may have been deliberately trying to hurt that person or just trying to speak your side of the situation. I've done this more times than I care to admit, and in the end, no matter what the reasons were, I always wish I could take those words back.

Whether we like it or not, our words can be like a spark in a dry forest. In minutes the damage can be done and everything is gone. Proverbs 26:20 says, "Without wood a fire goes out; without a gossip a quarrel dies down." We all want to be heard and tell our side, but at what cost?

My prayer is that we will ask the Lord to set a guard over our mouths and keep watch over the door of our lips. Only you can prevent forest fires . . .

Dear Jesus,
Thank you for Your Holy Spirit that whispers to my heart. Help me to be slow to speak and guard my words. Help me to . . .

The Invitation

Has God ever invited you somewhere? In 2016 He invited me to Israel, and I was overwhelmed.

This was my journal entry on 5-20-16: "If I ever thought I was in over my head, it is now, Lord. You invited me here, helped me pay, made the way, and now I am halfway and see so much more than I could have ever imagined. You are an awesome God, and I bless You. Please forgive me for just seeing one side of You, when You are like a diamond. You have so many facets and shine brighter than the sun. Please help me roll my life onto Your path, walk slowly and deliberately, and do Your will. Help me be Your disciple and to *Halak*—walk Your text. I love You, Lord!"

What is God inviting *you* to do? Believe in Him? Trust Him? Submit? Surrender? He gave us free will, so there is no coercion, only an invitation. What will happen if you say yes? I said yes and found myself in His country, surrounded by His voice, and I will never be the same. Whatever the invitation, surrender and say "Yes, Lord, here I am."

Dear Jesus,

Thank you for giving us free will. What a sweet invitation You have given me. Today I choose to roll my life onto Your path. Help me to . . .

A Slow Fade

It doesn't take much to walk off the path. We can easily get distracted by something, turn our eyes, and our feet will follow. As easy as it is to change direction, it can sometimes feel overwhelming to return.

And it doesn't always have to be moving toward something that is bad for us. Sometimes it can simply be moving away from God.

Many times I've set my alarm to get up, read the Bible, and spend time alone with God, only to find that after a couple of days I start hitting the snooze button, telling myself I'll do it tomorrow. But tomorrow turns into next week, which turns into next month, and I give up on getting up early, justifying that it's because life is busy and I need my rest. I feel the guilt seeping in and I pull away from God, building a wall to hide my shame.

The enemy loves that wall. He loves when we start to believe that God loves us only when we read His Word, only when we spend time alone with Him. That's not the truth. God loves us whether we spend time with Him or not, but He always wants us to. He wants to meet with you during the day or night. He wants you to read His Word because that is where we learn how to have a closer walk with Him. We must never stop trying, even when we get distracted, even when we step off the path. Don't believe the lies that it's too late. It's never too late to return.

Lamentations 3:40 says, "Let us examine our ways and test them, and let us return to the LORD."

Dear Jesus,

Forgive me when I walk away from You and thank you that I can always return. Help me to believe that You love me and want to spend time with me. Break down the walls in my life, especially the ones that the enemy helps me build. I love You, Lord. Help me today to . . .

Like Clay

There are 34 verses in the Bible about sculpting and clay. My favorite is Isaiah 64:8: "You, LORD, are our Father. We are the clay, you the potter; we are all the work of Your hand."

After I surrendered my life, to be what God had created me to be—I needed to be re-sculpted. I had so much sticking to me, so many things I had added that I thought were important, so many lies I had believed, and so many cracks and holes that needed to be repaired. I needed to be remade.

Even though it was a challenging process, I love that God didn't just stick a bandaid on me. He fixed the broken parts and made me into what he had originally designed me to be.

How about you? Are you masking your depression and pain from others? From God? I finally had to lay it all down at His feet and tell Him I couldn't go on. But He didn't just wave His hand over me and heal me. He went through each broken piece, each lie that I believed, and transformed me into a new creation. It wasn't overnight. It wasn't a quick fix. But it was permanent and forever!

It's never too late . . . you can start today. Be vulnerable with God and tell Him where you're hurting. Cry out to your Creator and ask to be made whole. Surrendering is the first step, followed by allowing Him to work on the areas of your life that need transformation. He will do amazing things!

Dear Jesus,

Thank you for loving me. Help me to surrender so You can fix in me whatever is broken. Help me to . . .

Community

The church I attended in my first marriage was a wonderful community. One year we held a revival and went to church every night for an entire week. We would share a meal together, a time of teaching, and songs of worship and praise. When the week started, it was challenging to arrange our schedule to go. But by Thursday it was such a joy to meet together as believers and worship. It gave me a beautiful picture of the early church: "Every day they continued to meet together in the temple courts. They broke bread in their homes and ate together with glad and sincere hearts, praising God and enjoying the favor of all the people" (Acts 2:46–47).

Do you have a church you belong to? If not, I encourage you to pray about it and ask the Lord to open doors for you to find a community of believers. We were designed to live in community with others, and to worship not only on Sunday but every day of our lives.

> "And let us consider how we may spur one another on toward love and good deeds, not giving up meeting together, as some are in the habit of doing, but encouraging one another—all the more as you see the Day approaching."
> —HEBREWS 10:24–25

Dear Jesus,

Thank you for designing me to live in community with others. Help me to worship You not only on Sunday but every day of my life. Help me to . . .

Daily Struggle

D o you ever wake up in the morning and ask the question *Why does my life have to be this hard?* I used to think for a long time that it was just me, that I was the only one struggling. But when I started to open my eyes to the truth, I saw that everyone has struggles. Everyone is going through something right at this very moment. They're experiencing a health issue, a financial trouble, a divorce, losing a loved one, losing a job, losing hope. The problem is that we live in a fallen world. We live in a dry desert, and Jesus is the One who can truly give us life. Until He comes again, we need to love and support each other, lifting each other up and bringing heaven here to earth.

> "If only for this life we have hope in Christ, we are of all people most to be pitied. But Christ has indeed been raised from the dead, the firstfruits of those who have fallen asleep."
> —1 CORINTHIANS 15:19-20

Whatever you're going through right now, know that you are not alone. Trust God with each day and give Him your struggles. He will walk with you.

Dear Jesus,
Some days it's hard to get out of bed and keep going. Everything seems overwhelming. But today, help me to give my struggles to You. Help me to realize that I am not alone and that You are walking with me. Today, help me to . . .

At the Corner of Lost and Confused

Have you ever stood at this corner? For those of you who don't know me, I was camped here for several years. In 1996 I was diagnosed with bipolar disorder, and over the next 17 years I would lose my marriage, go through bankruptcy, have health issues, believe every lie from the enemy, and carry around a bitterness that started to consume me. It wasn't until I surrendered to Jesus all of my hurt and pain and prayed over every area of my life that He healed me. Completely healed me! I am off all my medication and have been set free.

If you are standing at this corner today, know that there is hope. Whatever has brought you here, whatever pain you've been carrying, there is only one place you can go from here—to your knees. Trust that God can do amazing things with your life. I am living proof!

> "For everyone born of God overcomes the world. This is the victory that has overcome the world, even our faith. Who is it that overcomes the world? Only the one who believes that Jesus is the Son of God."
> —1 JOHN 5:4-5

Dear Jesus,

When I stand at this corner, I have no idea how You're going to help me. I can't see past my shame and heartache to the road ahead. Help me to trust You. I lay it all down at Your feet, all of my . . .

Forgive

We have all heard the saying "Refusing to forgive is like drinking poison and hoping it kills the other person." I know from personal experience how this feels. I sipped a poisonous concoction for months after I was remarried, trying to get rid of the taste of bitterness. I felt justified. I felt that I was 100% right and my husband was wrong. But what I didn't realize was that my unforgiveness started to affect every other area in my life. I started to become bitter, and the poison sucked out the love, compassion, and joy I was meant to have in Christ. Sound familiar?

Matthew 6:14–15 says, "For if you forgive other people when they sin against you, your heavenly Father will also forgive you. But if you do not forgive others their sins, your Father will not forgive your sins."

Don't believe the lie that we are justified by the good things we do. Christ died for *all* of us while we were still sinners. Praise God that He did!

Dear Jesus,

Forgiveness isn't easy for me. I've been hurt so much in my life, it's hard to forgive and forget. But I'm humbled that You took my sin to the cross. Thank you. Help me to be more like You and forgive others. Help me to . . .

Directions to Happiness

Do you ever wish there were directions to happiness? The world tells us it has the answers: you just need to buy that house, or this car, or shop at that store. But these kinds of answers only bring emptiness—empty pockets and a hole inside you can never fill, no matter how much you spend.

In Matthew 6:19–21 Jesus says, "Do not store up for yourselves treasures on earth, where moths and vermin destroy, and where thieves break in and steal. But store up for yourselves treasures in heaven, where moths and vermin do not destroy, and where thieves do not break in and steal. For where your treasure is, there your heart will be also."

True happiness, my friends, comes from the Lord. Loving Him and obeying Him will bring you an indescribable peace. Following Him will bring you a life of adventure and fill the hole that is inside you. Trusting Him will allow you to have everything you need, in His timing and for His glory. Reading His Word will provide the only directions to happiness you will ever need. I'm praying that you believe this today!

Dear Jesus,

I struggle with being truly happy. I sometimes get caught up in all the things the world says I need. But let me find my true happiness in You. Help me to . . .

Trust

There was a time in my life when I had to completely trust that the Lord would provide. Back in 2007 I was laid off, and so was my ex-husband. The money he has been giving me all but stopped, and unemployment took forever to come. This was my first true test of believing that God was going to take care of myself and my children, with even the basic necessities like food and paying the heat and electric bills. Besides getting food from the church and help with paying my bills, some people would randomly stop by with groceries just at the right time. The love that I felt was overwhelming, and I knew that no matter what, God would provide. I needed to let go of how I thought it should be and trust in the way it was.

Jesus said, "'Therefore I tell you, do not worry about your life, what you will eat or drink; or about your body, what you will wear. Is not life more than food, and the body more than clothes? Look at the birds of the air; they do not sow or reap or store away in barns, and yet your heavenly Father feeds them. Are you not more valuable than they? Can any one of you by worrying add a single hour to your life?'" (Matthew 6:25–27).

Dear Jesus,

There are some days I'm not sure how it's all going to come together. But when I fool myself into thinking I'm in control, I feel like I can make it happen. Help me to trust You! Help me to let go of the reins and know that You love me and only want what's best for me. Help me to . . .

What Is Your Drug of Choice?

My question for you today is this: What is your drug of choice? I believe all of us at one time or another have used something to get us through the day. It may be alcohol, drugs, food, television, shopping, medication, and the list goes on and on. Are you still doing this, using something to mask your pain? If you are, the enemy is winning. You are believing a lie that you need this and that God is not enough. Our hope cannot be in the things of this world that only numb our pain for a time. Our true hope is in Jesus Christ, who loves us and promises to take all our pain and sorrow and wipe away every tear from our eyes.

If you need help, you can join a local recovery group or reach out to a friend or family member. You can reach out to me at info@ammiebouwman.com.

It is my prayer that today you will take the first step forward by recognizing if you have a drug of choice and giving that over to Jesus. He will grab your hand and help you take the next step . . . and the next. I'm praying for you today, my friend.

Dear Jesus,
Help me today to admit if I'm using something other than You or Your Word to get through my day. Help me to trust You with all of my pain, all of my heartache, all of my anxiousness. Help me to . . .

God's Truth

You'll never get through this.

No one loves you.

Stop trying.

You are a nobody.

And the lies go on and on . . .

The truth is that the enemy is a liar. The truth is that the enemy (the devil) is here to steal and destroy, prowling around like a roaring lion, looking for someone to devour. The truth is that he is constantly whispering lies to us and that when we start to believe them it will affect our clarity of mind, our relationships, our jobs, and our ability to trust God. The truth is that it's never too late to rebuke the cold whisper in your ear and command him to get behind you in the powerful name of the Lord Jesus Christ! Start believing the truth. The truth is that you will get through to the other side. The truth is that you are loved so much that Jesus died for you. The truth is you are God's child, and that makes you a son or daughter of the King!

Stop believing the lies, my friend. Declare this truth today and make it your own! Amen!

Dear Jesus,

I have heard these lies, and I have believed them. Help me to believe Your truth. Help me to rebuke the enemy and be confident of who I am in You. Strengthen me and . . .

Be Still and Know

"Be still, and know that I am God."
—PSALM 46:10

This has been my life verse. When my mind was racing. When I got laid off from my job. When my cupboards were empty and I stood in line at the food pantry. When my house was foreclosed. When I signed the divorce papers. When I didn't know where to turn. He reminded me that He is God! He quieted my heart with these words, and I knew that He was bigger than my situation.

Whatever you are going through right now, be reminded today that God is God! He will quiet your heart and give you peace in this moment.

Thank you, Father, for loving me, walking with me, and never giving up on me. Amen.

Dear Jesus,
You know my struggles. You know what I'm going through right now. Help me to be still and know that You are God. Help me to . . .

The Battle Is Real

I don't know about you, but there are days when I feel like I'm in a battle for my life. I feel like I'm dodging bullets of discouragement, arrows of sadness, nets of lies . . . and I've had it! The battle is real, my friends. The enemy will not take my happiness, my freedom, my pursuit of the kingdom of God, and you should not let him take yours. Starting today, put on the full armor of Christ. Pray each day for wisdom to know the truth. Pray for your friends and your loved ones and those who are suffering. Pray for strength. We will not give up because we are the sons and daughters of the risen King! This means war . . .

Dear Jesus,

Thank you for loving me. Give me strength for this day to battle the enemy. Help me to put on Your full armor and fight. Help me to . . .

Asking God a Question

Have you ever asked God a question? I have, when I was 19 years old. As I grew more and more serious with the guy I was dating, I asked God "Is this the right path? Is he the one for me?"

I heard a still, small voice inside, saying, "No."

But no was not the answer I was prepared for, and thinking about leaving him was more than I could bear. I loved him. I didn't want to listen. I had fallen so hard and so deep you could no longer see the top of my head. The ground had opened up and I was gone.

I chose the man over God's answer, and God never brought it up again. The sad thing was that God knew the life I would have by choosing this man. He knew the pain and suffering, and how long it would last. I was still loved by God, and He blessed me with two beautiful children, but what would my life have looked like now had I listened and obeyed?

It is not easy to give up things we think we want. But to trust God means you have to trust His answers, even when they're no. Next time you ask God a question, be open to whatever His answer may be, and trust that He has your best interests in mind and heart.

Dear Jesus,
Please forgive me for the times I heard Your answer but didn't listen.
Help me to be obedient to Your will. Help me to . . .

The Prisoner

When Paul wrote Philippians, he was sitting in a prison in Rome. Paul knew it wasn't about the situation he was in; it was about the work Jesus was doing in and through him in that season of his life.

We have all been in some kind of prison: a prisoner of a situation, a lifestyle, an addiction—even a prisoner of our mind. But we need to have hope that God is not done with us yet. Let Him finish the work in you. He will break your chains and give you the kind of freedom that can only be found in Him, and a prize of everlasting life.

> "Not that I have already obtained all this, or have already arrived at my goal, but I press on to take hold of that for which Christ Jesus took hold of me. Brothers and sisters, I do not consider myself yet to have taken hold of it. But one thing I do: Forgetting what is behind and straining toward what is ahead, I press on toward the goal to win the prize for which God has called me heavenward in Christ Jesus."
> —PHILIPPIANS 3:12-14

Dear Jesus,
Let me be open to the work You have yet to do in me. Break these chains that stop me from being free. Help me to claim Your promises and . . .

Be Careful What You Think and Believe

Proverbs 4:23 says "Above all else, guard your heart, for everything you do flows from it." I know this to be true because there was a time I thought I was dying. Every day I struggled with aches and pains, feeling tired and overwhelmed by the feeling that something was wrong. Everything revolved around my health and what I thought was going on.

What I didn't know at the time was that the enemy had found a way to paralyze me with my thoughts. I couldn't move forward—I couldn't even move sideways. I hit a wall and couldn't see the truth.

Is there something you believe about yourself or others? Is it truth? Ask God to reveal it to you and to rebuke the enemy. Life is too short to waste precious time believing lies and not living this gift of life to the fullest.

Dear Jesus,

Help me to guard my thoughts and only to believe Your truths. Help me to stop believing the lies of the enemy. Help me to stand on Your firm foundation and know . . .

The Line in the Sand

There comes a time in our lives when we need to decide. This is where we draw the line in the sand, my friends, where we decide to whom we belong.

First John 2:15–17 says, "Do not love the world or anything in the world. If anyone loves the world, love for the Father is not in them. For everything in the world—the lust of the flesh, the lust of the eyes, and the pride of life—comes not from the Father but from the world. The world and its desires pass away, but whoever does the will of God lives forever."

To make the decision to follow Jesus seems like it's hard and that you will have to give up so much. But that is the lie. Living for and loving Jesus is like breathing. It's what we were designed for. When you cross that line, you are crossing into forever . . . an eternity with Jesus. He has done all the work; all you have to do is trust and believe.

Today, draw the line and cross it. Into His arms, into His grace, into a life He has designed for you all along.

Dear Jesus,
Today I choose You. Today I tell You with a loud voice that I love You and want to belong to You alone. I'm crossing the line into Your arms. Help me to . . .

The Diagnosis

I've been told I am lucky. But luck has not saved me. A hand pulled me up from the dark, deep pit that held my soul so tight there was not a bit of air left in my lungs. Each day I traveled down a road with no streetlights, that had houses with no doors and rooms with no windows. To the world I was fine, but in my own mind I couldn't slow the racing thoughts or get off the roller coaster of highs and lows that would dip and turn, leaving me frantically cleaning my home or staying in bed with the breakfast and lunch dishes on the counter. In the early part of 1996 I was diagnosed with bipolar disorder. This is a manic-depressive disorder categorized as mental illness. I lived in a fog, not in touch with reality or aware of who I really was.

Have you ever been diagnosed with something that changed your entire life? Have you ever hated your circumstances so much that the only out you could see was ending it all? I'm here to tell you there is hope. God is bigger than bipolar disorder, depression, heart disease, cancer, marital problems, and all the other painful circumstances we face every day. We were created to have a relationship with God, to live with Him and enjoy this beautiful creation. But when sin entered the world everything became broken. Don't believe the lies of the enemy, the one that opened the door for sin to come in. He's here to kill and destroy and keep you from having a relationship with God. Remember, *you* are a child of God, and you are loved.

Dear Jesus,

Thank you for loving me. Thank you that You are bigger than my circumstances, and that You walk with me even in the darkness. Help me today to . . .

Bankrupt

In 2002 we had backed ourselves so far into the corner with our debt that there was no longer a space big enough to stand. We were left with one painful decision: bankruptcy. We had tried everything to fix the years of intractable poor choices we had made. We had even hired a debt consolidation company to try to get us back on track. But after spending an additional $3,000, we still declared bankruptcy. It was a waste. One afternoon I stood in the kitchen after countless calls from creditors and tried to balance a checkbook with no money. With hands raised and nothing left to offer the world, I cried out to God.

"Lord, I give up. I'll do whatever you ask. But I can't do this on my own anymore." I remember feeling a weight lifting from my shoulders, as though I were taking off my backpack and laying it down after a long journey. I somehow trusted that it was going to be okay, although I had no idea how He would fix the mess that we had gotten ourselves into or what He would ask me to do. The first thing He asked me to do was give up my pride, because we would have to give it all back. We declared bankruptcy and started over, and I was ready to trust God and follow Him wherever He would lead me . . . which brings me to you. If you're reading this today and are in a similar situation, you need to surrender. Throw up your arms and tell God you can't do this without Him anymore. He will show you the way, just as He showed me.

Dear Jesus,

I give up. I'll do whatever You ask. I surrender to You my brokenness, my pride, my control. I can't do this without You anymore. Help me to . . .

Count It All Joy

*"Consider it pure joy, my brothers and sisters, whenever you
face trials of many kinds, because you know that the testing
of your faith produces perseverance."*

—JAMES 1:2–3

Do you know who James was? He was the son of Mary, a brother to Jesus. James wrote this letter to the scattered Jewish believers to make this point: as expressed by Steven J. Cole, "True faith shows itself in practical, godly living."

While it is hard to have joy in the trial, this is something we must work toward. When we look back, over our pain, over our regret, over our mistakes and missed opportunities, we will find that our joy was given to us by God, and that in the process we were shaped to be more like Jesus. God never promised that this life would be easy, only that He would never leave us nor forsake us. He is refining us with fire so that someday we can stand on streets of gold. Amen!

Dear Jesus,
Thank you for loving me. Help me to have joy in these trials. Help me follow You. Help me to . . .

February

LEAVING EGYPT FOR THE PROMISED LAND

"I am the LORD, and I will bring you
out from under the yoke of the Egyptians.
I will free you from being slaves to them,
and I will redeem you with an outstretched arm
and with mighty acts of judgment."

–EXODUS 6:6–7

Moses

I think that most people, regardless of their faith, have heard of Moses. He's the man who brought the Israelites out of Egypt and led the people across the Red Sea on dry ground. But did you know that Moses was born during a time when by the law of Pharaoh every Hebrew baby boy who was born was to be killed? The Egyptians were worried that the Israelites would eventually outnumber them and join their enemies and fight against them.

But God had such an extraordinary plan for Moses' life that he was spared. Baby Moses was taken to the Nile River by his sister, hoping that he would be found—which he was, by Pharaoh's daughter! God even orchestrated that his own mother could nurse him and be paid to do so. When he grew older, he lived in the palace as the son of Pharaoh's daughter.

Moses had a privileged life living as an Egyptian, until he saw an Egyptian and a Hebrew fighting. Moses killed the Egyptian and fled to the desert in fear for his life. Again, God put Moses on a path, preparing him for what God had in store.

As we look ahead to our promised land, we realize that we don't always know what's before us. But we will need to be obedient for the journey ahead.

Dear Jesus,
Thank you that You have a path for me. Help me to obedient in the journey. Help me to . . .

Moses and the Burning Bush

In the desert Moses met the woman Zipporah, the daughter of Jethro, and married her. One day when Moses was tending sheep, he saw a burning bush that did not burn up. As he approached, God spoke to him.

> "When the LORD saw that he had gone over to look, God called to him from within the bush, 'Moses! Moses!'
>
> And Moses said, 'Here I am.'
>
> 'Do not come any closer,' God said. 'Take off your sandals, for the place you are standing is holy ground.'"
> —EXODUS 3:4–5

God told Moses that He had seen the misery of His people and was sending Moses to Pharaoh to bring His people out of Egypt. Even though Moses could see the miraculous sign of the burning bush and hear that God had a plan and was going to be with him, Moses was reluctant to do what God asked. He constantly said back to God, "Who am I? What if I can't do this? What if? What if? What if?" God even said Moses could take his brother, Aaron, with him for support and help, but Moses still doubted.

Has there ever been a burning bush in your life? Something that made you want to take a closer look, even though you went in the other direction? Today, remember that if God calls you to something, he will equip you for the task. No matter what it is.

Dear Jesus,

Thank you that You speak to me. Help me today to hear Your voice. Equip me for the journey. Help me to . . .

Moses Returns to Egypt

There are times when God asks us to go back. Back to a place in our life we left in haste. Back to a time when we were scared of the outcome. God did reassure Moses that all of the men who wanted to kill him were dead, so there was nothing to fear. But as he walked the long road back to Egypt, what were his thoughts? Did he focus on the past and all the things he could not do, or on his future, and that God was walking with him?

I know I can sometimes have a heavy heart when I return to a place I left on purpose. But God lovingly reminds me that I am His and that He is walking with me.

Today, if you need to go back, ask God to give you the strength you need and to remind you that there is nothing He cannot do.

Dear Jesus,
It's hard for me to go back. That part of my life is painful to think about and painful to relive. I pray for Your strength. Go before me and prepare the way. Help me today to . . .

God Promises Deliverance

When Moses and Aaron returned to Egypt and spoke to Pharaoh, Pharaoh became angry and told their slave drivers to not give away any more straw to the Israelites to make bricks. They would need to collect their own straw and still keep up their quota of bricks. The Israelites then became angry with Moses and Aaron, saying, "May the LORD look on you and judge you! You have made us obnoxious to Pharaoh and his officials and have put a sword in their hand to kill us" (Exodus 5:21).

When Moses returned to the Lord to tell Him what happened, he was discouraged and frustrated. But God said, "Now you will see what I will do."

God promised that He would bring the Israelites out from Egypt. That he would free them and bring them into the promised land.

Has God ever made you a promise? When He did, did you trust Him and His timing?

Dear Jesus,

Thank you for keeping Your promises. Help me today to trust You and Your timing. Help me to . . .

Leaving Egypt

Have you ever left for a trip, not sure where you are going or how long you would be gone—taking with you 2.4 million people? That was Moses when Pharaoh finally let them go. Egypt had experienced the ten biblical plagues, the final one being the death of every firstborn male in the land, from Pharaoh's house to that of the slave girl, to the cattle in the field. No one was untouched. When Pharaoh said to leave, the people of Egypt gave the Israelites food, clothing, jewelry, and gold and sent them on their way. Can you imagine the sheer numbers there were or the hours it would have taken them to exit the city? Leaving Egypt had to have been frightening and exhilarating, joyful and sad.

Can you imagine? Maybe you can because you have had to leave a place, knowing this was what God was calling you to do. But the promise of living with God in the promised land is what helped them put one foot in front of the other. They were leaving slavery behind and looking into the future of freedom.

Today, maybe you are starting a new journey. Ask God to give you the strength to follow where He leads, and to help you put one foot in front of the other as you leave for your promised land.

Dear Jesus,
Help me as I start this new journey. Give me the strength to put one foot in front of the other, and faith to follow You wherever You lead. Help me to . . .

The Red Sea

"When the king of Egypt was told that the people had fled,
Pharaoh and his officials changed their minds about
them and said, 'What have we done? We have let the
Israelites go and have lost their services!'"
—EXODUS 14:5

So Pharaoh took 600 of his best chariots and marched them toward the Israelites, who were camped by the Red Sea. God knew the Egyptians would follow. He had hardened Pharaoh's heart once again. "But I will gain glory for myself through Pharaoh and all his army, and the Egyptians will know that I am LORD'" (Exodus 14:4).

The Israelites were terrified and cried out to Moses. "'Was it because there were no graves in Egypt that you brought us to the desert to die?'" (Exodus 14:11).

But Moses stretched out his hand over the sea and God pushed back the waters so the Israelites could walk across on dry ground. And when the chariots came, the waters closed and swept them into the sea.

No matter what you are facing right now, there is nothing too big for God. We may not always understand what He is doing, but we do know that it is for His glory. He is the mighty God. Amen!

Dear Jesus,
Thank you that You always know what is best for me, even when I don't
understand. Help me today to trust You. Help me to . . .

Food and Water

Forty-five days into their journey . . . After the Israelites had watched the Lord part the Red Sea, they started to grumble about food and water. Each time the Lord provided, it was as though it weren't good enough and they wished they had been back in Egypt.

When I first read this, I was angry. How could this people live with God in community, see all these miraculous things, and still question whether He would provide? It was then that I was convicted. How many times have I seen God work in my life, only to doubt when things got challenging? I wasn't reading about the Israelites—I was reading about myself.

Father God,
Help us to trust You and Your provision. Open our eyes to see You living among us and providing for our every need. Please forgive us for wanting to return to a time when we were slaves to sin. Thank you for our freedom. Amen.

Dear Jesus,
Please forgive me for doubting You. Forgive me for the times I grumbled and wasn't content with Your gifts. Help me today to . . .

Jethro's Advice

When Jethro, Moses' father-in-law, had heard of everything that God had done for Moses and the people of Israel, He came to visit him, bringing with him Moses' wife, Zipporah, and their two sons.

Moses shared with him everything that had happened, and Jethro could see everything that Moses was doing for the people. It was then that Jethro gave Moses some advice: "'You must be the people's representative before God and bring their disputes to him. Teach them his decrees and instructions, and show them the way they are to live and how they are to behave. But select capable men from all of the people—men who fear God, trustworthy men who hate dishonest gain—and appoint them as officials over thousands, hundreds, fifties and tens'" (Exodus 18:19–21).

Why is Jethro's advice important enough for us to take notice? Because don't you love it when God brings people into our lives, usually outside of our situation, and they offer wisdom? They are able to see things objectively looking in, and to give us the kind of advice that will make a difference. Jethro could see that if Moses continued as he was he would not have the strength for the journey. He would need to surround himself with others who could help him carry the load of caring for the people.

Have you ever had someone step in and give you advice? Did you listen?

Dear Jesus,

Thank you that You always know what's best for me. Help me to have ears to listen when You speak into my life, especially through other people. Help me today to . . .

The Mountain

*"On the morning of the third day there was thunder and
lightning, with a thick cloud over the mountain, and a very
loud trumpet blast. Everyone in the camp trembled. Then
Moses led the people out of the camp to meet with God, and
they stood at the foot of the mountain. Mount Sinai was
covered with smoke, because the LORD descended
on it in fire. The smoke billowed up from it like smoke from
a furnace, and the whole mountain trembled violently.
As the sound of the trumpet grew louder and louder, Moses
spoke and the voice of God answered him."*

—EXODUS 19:16-19

I wish I could have been there on that day, before the glory of the Lord.
Can you put yourself there? The ground shaking below you, the smell of
smoke and heat, the sound of the trumpet in your ears. It would have been a
sensory overload for us and was probably the same for the Israelites. I think
we sometimes forget how big God is, and how powerful.

I pray that as we continue this month in the promised land, we'll
remember His glory and majesty from the mountain.

Dear Jesus,

*Thank you that You are the great I AM. Please forgive me when I put You
in a small box and forget how great You are. Today, let me experience
Your majesty. Open my eyes and help me to . . .*

The Ten Commandments

Without rules and boundaries in life, things can go considerably wrong. Before the Israelites get too far into their journey, I love how God gives them the Ten Commandments. He not only speaks to them from Mt. Sinai but writes on two stone tablets, using His own finger: "I am the LORD your God, who brought you out of Egypt, out of the land of slavery'" (Exodus 20:2).

And here, in abridged form, are the commandments He gave:

1. You shall have no other gods before me.
2. You shall not make idols.
3. You shall not take the name of the LORD your God in vain.
4. Remember the Sabbath day, to keep it holy.
5. Honor your father and mother.
6. You shall not murder.
7. You shall not commit adultery.
8. You shall not steal.
9. You shall not bear false witness against your neighbor.
10. You shall not covet.

The first four commandments tell us how God wants to be loved, and the last six show how to demonstrate love for other people. As you look at each one, how important are these commandments in your life? Are you following each one?

Dear Jesus,

Thank you for knowing what is best for me. Thank you for these commandments and how they give needed boundaries and protection to my life. Please forgive me for when I break them, especially when I . . .

The Golden Calf

When Moses was on Mt. Sinai for forty days and forty nights receiving the Ten Commandments and the directions for the tent of meeting, the Israelites were restless.

> "When the people saw that Moses was so long in coming down from the mountain, they gathered around Aaron and said, 'Come, make us gods who will go before us. As for this fellow Moses who brought us out of Egypt, we don't know what has happened to him.'"
> —EXODUS 32:1

After reading this, I had such a mixture of emotions: anger at the Israelites for not waiting, disgust over their golden calf image, and sadness, because I knew in my own heart that I have followed a golden calf in my life. We so long for physical evidence, something to see with our eyes. But what if our eyes fail us? Would we no longer be able to believe? True faith comes from inside us, in believing in Him more than in the proof we think we need.

Dear Jesus,

Thank you for loving me, even when You see me becoming restless. Help me, Lord, to have the kind of faith that does not need to see with my eyes. Help me to . . .

The Tent of Meeting/Temple

When I read the requirements for putting together the tent of meeting in 12 of the 40 chapters in Exodus, I was overwhelmed. There were so many intricate pieces and moving parts to bring it all together. But then I realized the extreme holiness of God and what He would need to live among His people. His love and patience for the Israelites was amazing.

But even more amazing was when Jesus died on the cross, and the temple was destroyed and the curtain separating the Most Holy Place (a place so sacred that only a priest was allowed in once a year) from the rest of the temple was torn in two. When Jesus died, all the requirements and logistics and moving parts were no longer needed. We now have full access to God with all of His holiness and can come to Him like a child comes to his father. Jesus bridged the gap.

Jesus,
We praise You for loving us so much that You died for us. Thank you for taking all of our sin and all of our shame to the cross. Thank you for bridging the gap so we can enter the full presence of God. We are forever thankful! Amen.

Dear Jesus,
Thank you. Thank you. Thank you! Help me to remember that I have this access to God and that I can approach His throne. Help me to . . .

The Offerings

When reading the first few chapters of Exodus, you will read about the many different kinds of offerings the Israelites needed to make before the Lord. There was the Burnt Offering, the Grain Offering, the Fellowship Offering, the Sin Offering, and the Guilt Offering. While I didn't understand the many offerings, I had made a note in the margin of my Bible that read "Hebrews 9:22" (this verse reads "Without the shedding of blood there is no forgiveness").

Until Jesus came, there needed to be offerings for our forgiveness. But His death on the cross has eliminated the need for anything else. He was the ultimate offering, washing away all of our sin with His own blood. We can rejoice! We are free!

"For Christ also suffered once for sins, the righteous for the unrighteous, to bring you to God. He was put to death in the body but made alive in the Spirit."
—1 PETER 3:18

Amen!

Dear Jesus,
Thank you for being the ultimate offering! Help me to confess my sins and be free! Help me to . . .

Quail from the Lord

Have you ever received a blessing from the Lord and then, after some time had passed, began to complain, saying, "This isn't what I expected!" I did, the first year into my second marriage. It was hard and challenging and not what I had expected, and I cried out to the Lord.

This is exactly what the Israelites exclaimed when they were tired of eating the manna: "'If only we had meat to eat! . . . But now we have lost our appetite; we never see anything but this manna!'" (Numbers 11:4, 6).

So the Lord gave them meat, and it came in the form of quail. And they ate it, not for one or two days but for a whole month until they couldn't stand it anymore.

When reading this passage, I was reminded that during that first year of my marriage I wasn't patient or grateful for my blessings. When we aren't grateful for His provisions on our journey, we lose sight of the lesson that "'man shall not live on bread alone, but on every word that comes from the mouth of God'" (Matthew 4:4).

Today, look deep into your life and see if there is something you're no longer grateful for. Have you questioned God's provision? His timing? His motives?

Dear Jesus,
Thank you for the way You provide for me! Help me to be content and to never lose sight of the lesson! Help me to . . .

The Promised Land

When Moses and the Israelites reached the promised land, God had them send men into the land to report back about the people who lived there and what the land was like and to bring back a sampling of the fruits that grew there. They were gone for forty days, and when they returned they gave their account: "'We went into the land to which you sent us, and it does flow with milk and honey! Here is its fruit. But the people who live there are powerful and the cities are fortified and very large'" (Numbers 13:27–28).

All the men but one said they should not enter the land, that the people were bigger and stronger than they were, and that they would surely die. All the people of the community began to cry out and lamented, "If only we had died in Egypt, or in this desert."

What do you do when you stand at the edge of the promised land that the Lord is giving you? Do you doubt His promises and think of a million reasons you shouldn't enter? Or do you step in with faith and anticipation of all the things the Lord will do? Today, think about your answer and ask God to speak clearly to your heart. Will you enter the promised land?

Dear Jesus,

Thank you for bringing me to the promised land! Help me not to be afraid of the unknown and to stand firm on Your promises. Help me to . . .

Forty Years

So the Lord replied to the grumbling, "'Not one of you will enter the land I swore with uplifted hand to make your home, except Caleb son of Jephunneh and Joshua son of Nun. As for your children that you said would be taken as plunder, I will bring them in to enjoy the land you have rejected. But as for you—your bodies will fall in this wilderness. Your children will be shepherds here for forty years, suffering for your unfaithfulness, until the last of your bodies lies in the wilderness. For forty years—one year for each of the forty days you explored the land—you will suffer for your sins and know what it is like to have me against you'" (Numbers 14:30–34).

I don't read this and think *What a cruel God!* I see the missed opportunity of standing at the threshold of a promise while still doubting, still complaining, still questioning after following Him who has proven Himself time and time again. I have stood in the desert, waiting to cross over and wanting to go back. But no more. I will trust Him wherever He leads, no matter the giants before me. What about you?

Dear Jesus,
Thank you for loving me, even when I doubt! Help me not to be afraid of the unknown, and to cross over into the promised land. Help me to . . .

Leaving the Mountain

Has God ever told you it was time to move on?

"In the fortieth year, on the first day of the eleventh month, Moses proclaimed to the Israelites all that the LORD had commanded him concerning them . . . , saying, The LORD our God said to us at Horeb, 'You have stayed long enough at this mountain.'"
—DEUTERONOMY 1:3, 5-6

When God told me it was time to leave, I sat overlooking the Maktesh Ramon in the Negev desert. I was on a trip to Israel to walk the text—a "bucket list" item that was not only a dream but a life transformation. It was here on this rock, looking down into the crater, that I heard God say it was time to tell my story to the world. When I came home I wrote my memoir, *In Over My Head*, and then *Living on the Waves*.

It has been an amazing journey so far, and I'm so glad I listened. I encourage you today, if God is saying it's time to leave, to step out in faith and leave your mountain. He will give you strength for your journey.

Dear Jesus,

Thank you for loving me! Open my ears so that I can hear You, and give me strength to be obedient. Help me to . . .

Do Not Forget the Lord

Before entering the promised land, Moses talked to the Israelites and reminded them of their journey: "'Remember how the LORD your God led you all the way in the wilderness these forty years, to humble you and test you in order to know what was in your heart, whether or not you would keep his commands. He humbled you, causing you to hunger and then feeding you with manna, which neither you nor your ancestors had known, to teach you that man does not live on bread alone but on every word that comes from the mouth of the LORD. Your clothes did not wear out and your feet did not swell during those forty years'" (Deuteronomy 8:2–4).

It's sometimes easy when things get back to normal and life is moving along smoothly to forget the Lord. This is what Moses did not want the people to do, and what we are not to do today. We must carry God in our hearts always, remembering what He has done for us and praising Him in the good times and the bad.

Today, if things are going smoothly, write down a list of things you are thankful for. Praise Him for this season. Do not forget the Lord.

Dear Jesus,

Thank you for Your many gifts! Help me to keep my eyes on You and praise You always; in the good times and bad. Help me to remember You when . . .

Crossing the Jordan

Imagine a raging river flowing at flood stage. It is wider and higher than normal and looks impossible to cross. Now imagine 2.4 million people waiting on one side of this river to cross into their promised land.

> "Yet as soon as the priests who carried the ark reached the Jordan and their feet touched the water's edge, the water from upstream stopped flowing. It piled up in a heap a great distance away, at a town called Adam in the vicinity of Zarethan."
> —JOSHUA 3:15-16

The whole nation crossed over, completely on dry ground. Does this surprise you? Sometimes God surprises me, but why should He? Time and time again He provides for us, holding back the waters so we can cross on dry ground. But just like the Israelites, we have to step in. We have to trust God and believe.

I pray that we will use this story as another reminder that nothing is too big for God. He promises us in this life, "When you pass through the waters, I will be with you; and when you pass through the rivers, they will not sweep over you. When you walk through the fire, you will not be burned; the flames will not set you ablaze. For I am the LORD your God" (Isaiah 43:2-3).

Dear Jesus,
Thank you for walking with me! Help me to believe that You are there, even in the deep waters. Help me to . . .

The Fruit of the Land

"On the evening of the fourteenth day of the month, while camped at Gilgal on the plains of Jericho, the Israelites celebrated the Passover. The day after the Passover, that very day, they ate some of the produce of the land: unleavened bread and roasted grain. The manna stopped the day after they ate this food from the land; there was no longer any manna for the Israelites, but that year they ate of the produce of Canaan."
—JOSHUA 5:10-12

Do you remember a time when you were able to enjoy the firstfruits of your labor? Maybe it was planting a garden, and after toiling each day in the soil—weeding, watering, and caring for the plants—you were able to eat your first tomato. The produce is sweet and satisfying and worth the long road to get there. I believe this was how it was for the Israelites. They had eaten manna for forty years while in the desert, and now they were partaking in the promise God had made to them. Their journey was long, but God was faithful.

Today, look into your own life and see where God has been faithful. Write out where you have seen answered prayer and thank Him for His provision.

Dear Jesus,
Thank you for being faithful! Help me to recognize Your fulfilled promises. Help me to . . .

Our Choices

*"'This day I call heaven and earth as witnesses against
you that I have set before you life and death, blessings and
curses. Now choose life, so that you and your children
may live and that you may love the LORD your God,
listen to His voice, and hold fast to Him.'"*
—DEUTERONOMY 30:19-20

I remember when I was younger reading something like this and thinking *Life or death? Is it really that serious?* But now that I'm older and have walked different paths to get to the one I'm on today, I know that it is. I know plenty of people who are alive but have lived a life of choices that didn't involve God, and their body and spirit are dying a slow death.

When God gives us the choice to love Him and serve Him, it is a gift, but He knows what will happen if we don't. We were made for Him, designed to be His children. Yet He gives us free will. And if we choose God, dying to self and living for Him, we will have everlasting life.

Dear Jesus,
Thank you for loving me! Thank you for the freedoms You give me and the boundaries You have set. Help me to remember that You know what's best for me. Help me to . . .

His Voice

There was a time, just as the Israelites did in the desert, when I hardened my heart toward the Lord. I asked him a question, and when the answer wasn't what I wanted to hear I did what I wanted anyway, and my decision came with incredible consequences. The Bible warns us against this in Hebrews 3:7–12, reminding us about the consequences the Israelites faced when they did not listen to God: "As the Holy Spirit says: 'Today, if you hear his voice, do not harden your hearts as you did in the rebellion, during the time of testing in the wilderness, where your ancestors tested and tried me, though for forty years they saw what I did. That is why I was angry with that generation; I said, "Their hearts are always going astray, and they have not known my ways." So I declared an oath in my anger, "They shall never enter my rest."' See to it, brothers and sisters, that none of you has a sinful, unbelieving heart that turns away from the living God."

I encourage you today to stay open to what the Lord says to you. Pray that you can hear His voice and be obedient to His will. If you do, you will have peace instead of negative consequences, joy instead of regret, love instead of shame, and the rest offered only by God the Father.

Dear Jesus,

Thank you for loving me! Thank you for forgiving me when I've hardened my heart against You. Help me to be obedient and listen to Your voice. Help me to . . .

Living in Our Past

Have you ever wanted to go back? Back to a place where even though there were pain and struggles it was safe and familiar and you knew what to expect? I once watched some old family movies on a lazy Saturday morning and was instantly drawn back in time. I could not only see my old life before my eyes in that video but could smell the dinner that was on the table and feel the chair I was sitting on. It was such a sensory overload that when I went to get up and shut it off I was dizzy and felt sick to my stomach.

All that day I wanted to go back. I wanted an opportunity to do that life over again and to incorporate all the things I now knew. But that wan't possible. I had relived one memory, one special moment in time, and when I remembered all of the other memories I was trying to forget I remembered why I had left. I remembered why the past needs to stay in the past, and why we have to live in the present.

I don't want to be like the Israelites, wanting to go back to slavery because that was familiar. I want to keep pressing into the unknown, into the promised land. What about you? Are you ready to cross over? Step out into the waters and feel God make a way for you to walk on dry land.

Dear Jesus,
Thank you for being patient with me, especially when I want to go back. But help me today to leave behind my past and cross over into the promised land. Help me to . . .

Idols

Have you ever wondered why God put such an emphasis on idols? In Exodus 20:22–23 He first mentions idols to the Israelites and then continues to express the necessity of keeping them out of their lives: "Then the LORD said to Moses, 'Tell the Israelites this: "You have seen for yourselves that I have spoken to you from heaven: Do not make any gods to be alongside me; do not make for yourselves gods of silver or gods of gold."'"

I remember thinking when I first read this, *I would never keep a gold idol in my possession.* But as the years went by there were several things I looked to instead of God: money, my husband, people's approval, myself.

God knew that we would easily be led astray if we didn't keep our eyes on Him. So the emphasis is a warning and a reminder of the snare it will be to us to have idols.

Is there anything in your life that you go to before God? Today, take an inventory. It's never too late.

Dear Jesus,

Thank you for loving me, even when I put things before You. Help me to recognize what I have allowed into my life that is a snare, and what I am relying on instead of You. Please forgive me, Lord. Help me to . . .

Stiff-Necked

The definition for *stiff-necked* is stubborn or inflexibly obstinate, as in stiff-necked pride or a stiff-necked people. The term was used by God to describe the Israelites several times in the exodus story, and as a way to alert other people in the Bible by looking back to the way the Israelites had acted in the desert.

I myself have been described as stiff-necked (stubborn) and still struggle with levels of that today. When I get an agenda in my head, I need to make sure that it's not mine, but God's. I need to remind myself to be flexible and trust the road I'm on. It may be uncomfortable at times, but I'm walking toward God's promise.

Are you stiff-necked? If you are, ask God to soften your heart and help you be obedient and to keep you on the right path into the promised land.

Dear Jesus,
Thank you for loving me, even when I'm stiff-necked. Soften my heart, and help me to be obedient to what You have planned for me. Help me to . . .

The Jar of Manna

*"So Moses said to Aaron, 'Take a jar and put an omer
of manna in it. Then place it before the Lord
to be kept for the generations to come.'"*
—EXODUS 16:33

Why do you think God wanted the manna in a jar? Could it be that He wanted the generations to come to have a reminder of how He had provided for His people in the desert? It would be a great conversation starter, wouldn't it? "What's in the jar?"

But what about in this day and age? Do we have something we can point people to and say "This is what God did for me"?

Sometimes we need those reminders ourselves—a way of looking back and seeing how far we've come and how God has walked with us. Maybe it's a jar or a prayer journal, a way to record our blessings and answered prayers. Either way, I encourage you to start such a record today. You will be amazed to see all the ways God shows up day after day, just as He did with the manna.

Dear Jesus,

Thank you for answering prayers. Thank you for being the ultimate reminder that we can look to You and see what You did for us. Thank you for dying on the cross and giving me new life. Help me to see all the ways You work in my life. Help me to . . .

God's Prediction

Did you know that God knew? God knew that when the Israelites got into the promised land they would forsake Him and worship the gods of the land. "'When I have brought them into the land flowing with milk and honey, the land I promised on oath to their ancestors, and when they eat their fill and thrive, they will turn to other gods and worship them, rejecting me and breaking my covenant'" (Deuteronomy 31:20). And yet He took them anyway. When I read that I was overcome with emotion. Why would He do that? Why would He go through so much to have a relationship with a people who would just turn around and forsake Him in the end?

But then I realized He's still doing that today. He's still reaching out to us, walking with us, and staying with us when we are obedient, . . . and when we turn our faces away. He has not changed. For that I am thankful and love Him all the more.

But I am reminded that the Bible gives us not only a prediction but a promise, telling us that one day Jesus will return. Our time here is fleeting, and if we are not ready we will be left behind. Are you ready? Are you living a life that is ready for His return, or are you wandering in the desert? It's not too late. Surrender your life and step into the promised land.

Dear Jesus,
Thank you for Your faithfulness. I am ready to stop wandering in the desert and follow You into the promised land. Help me to surrender my life. Help me to . . .

The Promised Land

All month long we have been talking about leaving Egypt and entering the promised land. Has anything stirred within you? Has God spoken to your heart, revealing things in your life that it is time to lay down? Reminding you that you cannot live by bread alone, but on every word that comes from the mouth of the Lord? If He has, let Him know today that you're listening. Ask Him to help you renew your commitment to follow Him out of the desert and into the life He has prepared for you. It's not too late. Tell Him today . . .

Dear Jesus,

Thank you for this day. Thank you for what You've shown me this month and whispered to my heart. I want to commit my life and follow You. I want to worship You and praise You in the good times and bad. I want to trust all that You have for me and step out into faith. Help me, Lord. Help me to . . .

March

WHY LENT?

"'Even now,' declares the LORD,
'return to me with all your heart, with fasting
and weeping and mourning.' Rend your hearts
and not your garments. Return to the LORD your God,
for he is gracious and compassionate,
slow to anger, and abounding in love,
and he relents from sending calamity."

–JOEL 2:12–13

Observing Lent

My first season of "observing" Lent was back in 2013. I went to an Ash Wednesday service and learned that the season of Lent was designed to evaluate areas in your life where you were thirsting for God.

At the time my thoughts went to my struggling marriage, and I spent the next two weeks realizing that I was full of bitterness and resentment toward my husband and could no longer push those feelings aside. They were actually choking out the love. Through prayer I was able to see the areas that I needed to change, which in turn changed my marriage.

Since then I've embraced Lent and used it as time to reflect on my life and how I can grow closer to God. Over these next forty days of Lent, we will start our journey toward the cross. We will be looking at prayer, Scripture, and other people's insightful views, with space to write your prayers and notes as you open your heart up to the Lord. All in the hope that we will embrace the greatest gift we were ever given.

Dear Jesus,
Give me strength as we start this journey to the cross. Prepare my heart for what You want to show me. Help me to know where I'm thirsting for You. Help me to . . .

What Does Lent Mean to You?

Before we spend the next forty days reflecting on Lent, what does Lent mean to you? Sometimes we may have a preconceived notion or idea that might inhibit us from experiencing everything God wants to show us.

I know I did. I thought Lent was all about giving something up. But what if it is more than that? What if it allows us to slow down to receive the greatest gift that was ever given— death on a cross to wipe away the debt for all humankind?

I challenge you to be open to what God wants to say to you these forty days. Pray this prayer with me:

Father God,
Thank you for loving us. Thank you for sending Your Son into this world to die for us. Thank you for bridging the gap so that we can have direct access to You. I pray that You will open our hearts to receive whatever You want to say to us. I pray that You will guard us with Your angels and put a hedge of protection around us to protect us from the enemy. Let us not believe his lies. Help us to be intentional in spending time with You. Give us ears to hear and wisdom to understand. In Jesus' name we pray these things, Amen.

Write out what Lent means to you. Any preconceived notions? Traditions from the past? Today, open up your heart and listen to the whisper of the Holy Spirit. Invite Jesus to reveal to you where you are thirsting for Him . . .

Dear Jesus,
Thank you for loving me. Thank you for wanting a closer relationship with me. Help me to understand You more and understand what You did for me. Help me to . . .

Jesus in the Wilderness

In a blog post by Gary Dorrien from the *Huff Post*, he writes, "Lent is the time when we think of Jesus in the wilderness. The gospel of Mark is short and vivid on this topic: 'He was in the wilderness 40 days, tempted by Satan; and he was with the wild beasts; and the angels waited on him.' . . . Matthew and Luke elaborate on the temptations. In their telling, Jesus was tempted by Satan with food to overcome his hunger; tempted to jump from the pinnacle of the temple, to prove he was the Son of God; and tempted to claim dominion over the world."

If you've ever thought that Jesus doesn't know what we go through as humans, this is just another reminder that He does. And I don't think it's any coincidence that He spent forty days in the wilderness—forty days struggling with the same things we all struggle with today.

While we may not struggle with true hunger, we hunger for love and affirmation. While we're not asked to jump from the tallest building to prove who we are, we are put into situations where we're asked to prove our loyalty, our worth, whether we're "cool" enough, or whether we have what it takes. And while we're not asked to bow down and worship someone with worldly power, we are asked to forget what we believe in for others' approval.

So, to follow His example, no matter what we go through in this life we need to draw our strength from God the Father. We need to know that people do not live on bread alone, that we are to worship the Lord our God and serve Him only, and that we are not to put the Lord our God to the test.

Dear Jesus,

It's hard for me to understand that You know what I go through on a daily basis. It's hard for me to understand that You were tempted in the wilderness and had to listen to the lies of the enemy. I hear his lies every day, Lord. I struggle with knowing the truth. Help me to follow Your example. Help me to stand on Your truth. Help me today to . . .

There Is Freedom in Forgiveness

Forgiveness. Is this something you need to give in this Lenten season? Is there someone who has wronged you? Is there someone who has hurt you physically or mentally, and is this a burden you carry around every day?

Or maybe you have wronged someone, and you need to let them know how sorry you are.

There are three words that can diffuse a situation, and three other words that can set you free, depending on your role: *I forgive you* and *I am sorry*. Forgiving others can be a challenging thing. But Jesus said in Matthew 6:14–15, "'If you forgive other people when they sin against you, your heavenly Father will also forgive you. But if you do not forgive others their sins, your Father will not forgive your sins.'"

While forgiving someone can be hard, it can be just as hard humbling ourselves before someone and saying "I am sorry" and admitting we were wrong. Paul writes in 2 Corinthians 7:9, "Yet now I am happy, not because you were made sorry, but because your sorrow led you to repentance. For you became sorrowful as God intended and so were not harmed in any way by us."

Repentance—that is the key to true freedom. Today, ask Jesus to help you work on asking for forgiveness, forgiving others, and accepting the sweet forgiveness Jesus offers you.

Dear Jesus,

Thank you for this day. Help me, Lord, to humble myself and ask for forgiveness, and to be able to forgive others as You forgive me. Help me today to . . .

The Lost Sheep

Luke recounts Jesus' words in Luke 15:4–7: "'Suppose one of you has a hundred sheep and loses one of them. Doesn't he leave the niney-nine in the open country and go after the lost sheep until he finds it? And when he finds it, he joyfully puts it on his shoulders and goes home. Then he calls his friends and neighbors together and says, "Rejoice with me; I have found my lost sheep." I tell you that in the same way there will be more rejoicing in heaven over one sinner who repents than over ninety-nine righteous persons who do not need to repent.'"

This parable isn't really about lost sheep. It's about how Jesus will earnestly seek us when we're lost and rejoice when He brings us home. There is a song called "Reckless Love" that sings about just this. He loves us with a reckless love. He would do anything for us to find us and bring us back to Him. He leaves the ninety-nine to find us and bring us home. And nothing we do can earn His love.

My question for you today is Are you lost? Jesus is earnestly seeking you right now. Cry out to Him, and let Him know you are ready to be found.

Dear Jesus,
Thank you for not giving up on me. Thank you for leaving the ninety-nine to find me. Help me, Lord, to . . .

The Punishment We Deserve

Ron Rand writes in *For Fathers Who Aren't in Heaven*:

"Michael usually takes his family out each week to see a movie or sports event. When they come home, they make a fire in the fireplace and pop popcorn.

During one of these evenings, little Billy made a real pest of himself in the car on the drive home, so he was punished by being sent to sit in his bedroom while the rest of the family had popcorn. After the family had the fire going and the popcorn ready, Michael went back to Billy's room and said, 'You go out with the others. I'll stay here and take your punishment.'

Through Michael's action, the entire family experienced a vivid example of what Jesus did for everyone."

Would you be willing to do that? Take someone else's punishment? That's what Jesus did. He was innocent and pure and yet died a cruel death in our place.

Dear Jesus,

Thank you for taking my place. Thank you for Your sacrifice, and for taking the punishment I deserve. Help me to live each day in this gratefulness. I love You and I give You all the praise and glory. Help me today to . . .

The Courage to Change

Maybe you've heard the saying "If you want to change, you have to be willing to be uncomfortable."

I think this is one of the hardest things we face when we're presented with change. It's the in between; it's the unsettled, uncomfortable feeling we have until we get to the other side and it becomes our new normal. But if we're not willing to be uncomfortable, we'll never grow and never experience the fullness of life God has in store for us.

Ask God right now if He will prepare your heart and give you the courage for whatever He is asking you to change.

Dear Jesus,

It's uncomfortable to think about change. I'm afraid. What if people don't like the new me? Help me, Lord, to be obedient to whatever You ask of me, and give me strength to face whatever You show me. Help me to . . .

A Fallen World

It seems that, as of late, there have been a lot of hard times. From fires out West to earthquakes to hurricanes. And this is on top of all the other things we are already dealing with as families, communities, and across the globe. But we must not forget that even though we are living in a fallen world, God is still God and He loves us. Keep trusting Him even in the hard times.

> "God is our refuge and strength,
>   an ever-present help in trouble.
> Therefore we will not fear, though the earth give way
>   and the mountains falls into the heart of the sea."
> —PSALM 46:1-2

Today's truth: We live in a fallen world. This was not God's design—not death, disease, famine, poverty, human trafficking, war . . . and the terrible list goes on and on. We were designed to live with Him, but when sin entered the world everything changed. Know the truth, stay in His Word, and remember to whom you belong!

Dear Jesus,
Help me, Lord, to not fear but to trust in You. Help me to have courage in the hard times and to know that You are walking with me. Help me to . . .

Deep Waters

A re you walking through rivers of difficulty right now? If so, cry out to the Lord. Let Him know that you are afraid or angry or that you can't take another step without Him. Reach for His hand. He will save you.

"But now, this is what he LORD says—
 he who created you, Jacob,
 he who formed you, Israel:
'Do not fear, for I have redeemed you;
 I have summoned you by name; you are mine.
When you pass through the waters,
 I will be with you;
and when you pass through the rivers,
 they will not sweep over you.
When you walk through the fire,
 you will not be burned;
 the flames will not set you aablaze.
For I am the LORD your God,
 the Holy One of Israel, your Savior.'"
—ISAIAH 43:1-3

Dear Jesus,

Thank you for this day. Thank you for the breath in my lungs and that You woke me up this morning. Help me, Lord. I am drowning and I need You. Please take my hand and . . .

Three Wishes

Today's truth: God is not a genie in a bottle. Every time we want something we can't just cry out to Him and expect Him to grant our wishes—and then get mad at Him when he doesn't. He knows what's in our heart and the motive behind our asking. Psalm 91:14–16 states, "'Because he loves me,' says the LORD, 'I will rescue him; I will protect him, for he acknowledges my name. He will call on me, and I will answer him; I will be with him in trouble, I will deliver him and honor him. With long life I will satisfy him and show him my salvation.'"

It's not about the things God could give us but about the relationship we can have with Him. Today, let's evaluate our relationship and make sure we're right with Him.

Dear Jesus,

Thank you for this day. Forgive me for coming to You only when I want something. What I really want is to have a relationship with You, Lord. Help me to . . .

Behind Every Door

Do you have rooms in your heart where you have closed the door to God? Do you say each day, "You can't go in there, Lord. It's too messy. I need to straighten some things up before I let you in there. Just stay in this room where it's clean"? Did you know that was another lie? Even though we think we can keep things from God, we can't. He knows everything! He knows what's behind every door in our heart, and He longs for us to share it with Him. He wants to help.

I would urge you, no matter what you're facing today or going through right now, to not take another step without asking Jesus for help. It's never too late to surrender your life, stop believing the lies of the enemy, and live for Him. It doesn't matter what you've been hiding from Him. He already knows, and He wants to help you. He will take you by your hand and walk with you into the life He has designed for you all along.

> "Therefore, if anyone is in Christ, the new creation has come. The old has gone, the new is here!"
> —2 CORINTHIANS 5:17

Dear Jesus,
Thank you for this day. Help me, Lord, to allow You into every room in my heart. Please forgive me for keeping things from You. Help me to . . .

The Enemy Is Real

Don't be surprised that when you start thinking and praying about change the enemy will be right at your heels, reminding you of your past and whispering discouragement and lies. Don't believe the lies, my friends, and when he reminds you of your past, remind him of his future.

> "Be alert and of sober mind. Your enemy the devil prowls around like a roading lion looking for someone to devour. Resist him, standing firm in the faith, because you know that the family of believers throughout the world is undergoing the same kind of sufferings."
> —1 PETER 5:8–9

Dear Jesus,
Help me, Lord, to be strong and watch out for the enemy. Help me to . . .

The True Vine

I remember when I made the decision to let God completely work in my life, pruning the areas that were dead and clearing out the overgrown weeds. When He was done, the Son could shine on every area in my heart, and I was transformed. And He can do the same for you . . .

> "'I am the true vine, and my Father is the gardener. He cuts off every branch in me that bears no fruit, while every branch that does bear fruit he prunes so that it will be even more fruitful. You are already clean because of the word I have spoken to you. Remain in me, as I also remain in you. No branch can bear fruit by itself; it must remain in the vine. Neither can you bear fruit unless you remain in me.'"
>
> —JOHN 15:1–4

Dear Jesus,

Thank you for this day. Please prune in me the dead places and clear out those areas overgrown with weeds so I can produce fruit. Please help me to remain firmly planted in You and to . . .

Be a Light

"This is the message we have heard from him and declare to you: God is light; in him there is no darkness at all. If we claim to have fellowship with him and yet walk in the darkness, we lie and do not live out the truth. But if we walk in the light, as he is in the light, we have fellowship with one another, and the blood of Jesus, his Son, purifies us from all sin.

If we claim to be without sin, we deceive ourselves and the truth is not in us. If we confess our sins, he is faithful and just and will forgive us our sins and purify us from all unrighteousness. If we claim we have not sinned, we make him out to be a liar and his word is not in us."

—1 JOHN 1:5-10

Dear Jesus,
Help me, Lord, to be a light that shines brighter than the darkness. To be a calm amidst the storms of this world. To be love to those around me who need Love and to shine brightly for those who need to see You through me. Please forgive me for my sins and help me to walk with You. Amen.

Dear Jesus,
Thank you for this day. Help me, Lord, to . . .

Moving Sale

I drove by a moving sale the other day. They had signs out by the yard inviting people in to see all of their household items for sale. There were cars parked in the driveway and people walking in and out. I wondered how it would feel to set out all of my earthly possessions in hopes of selling them, and I wondered how it would feel to have people come into my home and buy the things I held most dear.

It wouldn't matter if this was a necessity because I needed the money or was taking on a Grand Adventure and was hopeful of purchasing new items when I arrived at my destination. I can imagine it would feel the same. Vulnerable. Nostalgic. Numbing. Watching as each item left my home.

I then went one step further . . . What if we invited God into our hearts, asking Him to take out the things we needed to let go of? All of those things have already been purchased . . . on the cross. Our regret, our transgressions, our past. What would it feel like to live that way—not hanging on, no luggage, allowing God easy access into our hearts? Would I be willing to do that? I think the answer at times would be no.

Today I pray that the Lord will help us hang on loosely to the things of this world. I pray that we will invite Him into every area of our life, especially the parts that we hang onto: the past, the pain, our sin. I pray that He can walk freely through the open front door and move throughout our hearts.

Dear Jesus,

Thank you, Lord, that You love me in spite of my sin. Thank you that You walk with me when I'm afraid and stand in front of me when I need protection. Thank you for Your words of truth when the enemy screams loudly in my ears. Help me today to open wide the door of my heart. Come in and . . .

A Prayer of Confession

I know what it feels like, Lord, to step away from Your path and decide to travel my own way and leave You. I know what it feels like to make mistake after mistake, traveling further and further away until I'm cold and lonely and can no longer see You or see myself. So today I cry out to You. Please hear me and wrap me in Your arms. Help me find the right road that brings me back to You. I love you, Lord, and I am so grateful for Your mercy, forgiveness, and unending love. I am home. Amen.

Dear Jesus,

Help me, Lord, to lay it all down at the foot of Your cross. Help me to . . .

The Truth

Where do you find the Truth? I used to find my "truth" in the world. I used to listen to the people around me, following their ways and doing what they believed to be right. But everyone had a different view. Everyone believed in a different version of the "truth," and it was so confusing and challenging that my viewpoint changed daily. But, my friends, there is only *one* Truth, and it is found only in God's Word. He is consistent and never changing. Stay in His Word and you will know the Truth, and the Truth will set you free. Amen!

"'You are a king, then!' said Pilate.

Jesus answered, 'You say that I am a king. In fact, the reason I was born and came into the world is to testify to the truth. Everyone on the side of truth listens to me.'"
—JOHN 18:37

Dear Jesus,
Help me, Lord, to not listen to the world but to find the Truth in You.
Help me to . . .

Brick by Brick

Are you praying for God's discernment? Are you willing to be uncomfortable? He will tear down our walls of addiction and depression. He will tear down the walls we build around ourselves that separate us from family and friends. He will tear down the wall of lies that we believe every day, crippling us from change and the life God has prepared for us.

Keep the momentum going, my friend. Keep chipping away each brick until all you can see is sky. God will help you break through!

Dear Jesus,

Thank you for what You are doing in me. It's uncomfortable, but I can feel You walking with me. Lord, tear down my walls. Help me today to . . .

Choose Forward

We have all gone through experiences that have somehow shaped us or perhaps defined who we are today. Deciding whether or not you need to let go of your past is determining how much of your past is in your present.

Forward is the only way we can go. The Lord says, "I will instruct you and teach you in the way you should go; I will counsel you with my loving eye on you" (Psalm 32:8).

Today, make a choice to only go forward. Let go of what is in your past and know that it can no longer hurt you. Trust that God loves you and will walk with you.

> "Brothers and sisters, I do not consider myself yet to have taken hold of it. But one thing I do: Forgetting what is behind and straining toward what is ahead, I press on toward the goal to win the prize for which God has called me heavenward in Christ Jesus."
> —PHILIPPIANS 3:13–14

Dear Jesus,

Help me today to choose to go forward. Help me to let go of my past and trust that You are walking with me in my present and will be there in my future. Help me to . . .

Break Through

Do you see it? Once you break through your wall, the sky is clearer than it's ever been. The change that seemed overwhelming and uncomfortable is now behind you, and you realize that you didn't need that habit after all. God is the only thing we really need! Praise Him! Praise Him for showing you what areas in your life need to be pruned, what doors need to be opened, what rooms need to be cleaned. He wants you to let go the things of this world that aren't important. He wants you to let go of the lies and only believe the truth. He wants to have a relationship with you and to restore in you the desire to long for eternity, not the temporary things of this world.

Tell Him. Tell Him how you're feeling inside. Write down the questions of your heart, your praises of this week, your disappointments, your desires, and your dreams. Go to the Creator of the universe, the Father of your heart, your Comforter, your Friend, and let Him know how you feel.

Dear Jesus,
Thank you for today. I want to tell You . . .

Who He Is

In the words of H. Macgregor, "In adoration, we declare who He is! His awesome nature, what He does and all aspects of Him. We proclaim His nature, character and everything that makes Him good."

Some of the many names that chacterize and define Him . . .

Almighty
Counselor
I AM
Immanuel
Jehovah Jireh
Jesus
King of kings
Lord of Hosts
Savior
Teacher
Yahweh
Yeshua

Dear Jesus,

Thank you for this day. I praise You and lift Your name high. Thank you for . . .

Don't Give Up

I have noticed, now that we are halfway through, that it can be uncomfortable in this Lenten season, reflecting on the things God brings to our hearts. But I urge you, do not give up! Embrace this time, and be open to whatever He says to you. Each day now we get closer to the cross, and closer to the celebration that He lives!

Lord Jesus,
Please give me the courage to keep moving toward the cross. I am overwhelmed at what You did there for me and what You endured. Please empty me of all the things that are of me and fill me with You. Amen.

> "But God demonstrates his own love for us in this: While we were still sinners, Christ died for us."
> —ROMANS 5:8

Dear Jesus,
Thank you for the strength to keep going. I choose You, Lord! Even in this uncomfortable season, I choose to keep going so that I can be more like You. Help me, Lord, to . . .

Stay Focused

"In all this you greatly rejoice, though now for a little while
you may have had to suffer grief in all kinds of trials.
These have come so that the proven genuiness of your
faith—of greater worth than gold, which perishes even
though refined by fire—may result in praise,
glory and honor when Jesus Christ is revealed."

—1 PETER 1:6–7

Today, focus on the faithfulness of Christ. Where have you seen Him in your life? What prayers has He answered? What consistent truth have you heard from Him?

Dear Jesus,
Thank you for Your faithfulness. Help me to stay focused. Thank you for
speaking to my heart. I hear You, Lord. I hear You telling me . . .

Today Is a New Day

Today is a new day! I have regretted things in my life. And I remember the feeling I had before I gave those regrets to Jesus Christ. Regret had taken up residence and started to eat away at who I was. I physically hurt and could no longer escape the pain.

But there is good news! We have hope in Jesus Christ. Just as Paul did when he wrote these words in prison: "Brothers and sisters, I do not consider myself yet to have taken hold of it. But one thing I do: Forgetting what is behind me and straining toward what is ahead, I press on toward the goal to win the prize for which God has called me heavenward in Christ Jesus" (Philippians 3:13–14).

Open up your clenched fist and give God all of the regret you are holding onto. Today is a new day, and it is sweet!

Dear Jesus,

Thank you for today! Today, I open up my hand and lay before You all of my regret. Help me, Lord, to . . .

Fear

Is there something you are afraid of today? There are plenty of things in this world that can make us feel that way. But the feeling of fear is not from the Lord. He will give us peace, while the enemy will fill us with lies fueling the fear. Today I pray that you will recognize the difference and that, when you're fighting the battle between the two, Jesus will give you strength, wisdom, and clarity to step out and take His hand.

> "'For I am the LORD your God
>   who takes hold of your right hand
> and says to you, Do not fear;
>   I will help you.'"
> —ISAIAH 41:13

Dear Jesus,
I have been afraid. I've listened to the lies of the enemy and forgot that You are still in control. Help me, Lord, to conquer my fears. Help me to . . .

His Mercy

I know that once God showed me the changes I needed to make I was full of guilt and remorse for the years I had made the same mistakes. But even while He was rebuking and correcting me, He was whispering in my ear that He loved me, that He had redeemed me, and that I am His. And He feels the same way about you. Nothing can separate us from Him. He is the perfect Father.

Today, cry out to Him and repent and receive his loving whisper of forgiveness.

> "Have mercy on me, O God,
>> according to your unfailing love;
> according to your great compassion
>> blot out my transgressions.
> Wash away all my iniquiry
>> and cleanse me from my sin. . . .
>
> Create if me a clean heart, O God,
>> and renew a steadfast spirit within me.
> Do not cast me away from your presence
>> or take your Holy Spirit from me.
> Restore to me the joy of your salvation
>> and grant me a willing spirit, to sustain me."
> —PSALM 51:1-2, 10-12

Dear Jesus,

Thank you for Your unending mercy. Thank you for not giving me the punishment I deserve, but loving me unconditionally. Create in me a clean heart, Lord. Help me today to . . .

Return

Today and from this day forward don't believe the lies from the enemy. Nothing you have done is too big for God to forgive. You can always return. Each morning is filled with new mercies and His steadfast love.

"You have stripped off your old evil nature and all its wicked deeds. In its place you have clothed yourselves with a brand-new nature that is continually being renewed as you learn more and more about Christ, who created this new nature within you."
—COLOSSIANS 3:9–10

Dear Jesus,
Thank you for this day. I come before You in confidence today that You love me, that I am forgiven, and that You will never leave me. Help me to . . .

The Gate

R emember . . .

"Jesus said again, 'Very truly I tell you, I am the gate for the sheep. All who have come before me are thieves and robbers, but the sheep have not listened to them. I am the gate; whoever enters through me will be saved. They will come in and go out, and find pasture. The thief comes only to steal and kill and destroy; I have come that they may have life, and have it to the full.'"
—JOHN 10:7–10

Amen!

Dear Jesus,
Thank you that You are the gate. Thank you for protecting me and saving me. Help me, Lord, to listen to Your voice and know that . . .

His Love Never Fails

Even though there are times when we become painfully aware of our faults, let us remember that we are loved and that His love never fails.

> "Love is patient, love is kind. It does not envy, it does not boast, it is not proud. It does not dishonor others, it is not self-seeking, it is not easily angered, it keeps no record of wrongs. Love does not delight in evil but rejoices with the truth. It always protects, always trusts, always hopes, always perseveres. Love never fails."
> —1 CORINTHIANS 13:4–8

Dear Jesus,
Thank you that Your love never fails. Teach me to love like You. Help me, Lord, to . . .

I Have Decided to Follow Jesus

I know that change doesn't happen overnight. But there is one decision we can make and keep making every day when we open our eyes . . . that we are going to follow Jesus. We live in a world of things that will try to keep us from this, but if we keep our eyes on Him and keep making that decision our prize will be an eternity with Him! Today, make that decision!

> "I have decided to follow Jesus, no turning back, no
> turning back.
> The world behind me, the cross before me, no turning
> back, no turning back.
> Though none go with me, still I will follow, no turning
> back, no turning back.
> My cross I'll carry, till I see Jesus, no turning back, no
> turning back.
> Will you decide now to follow Jesus? No turning back, no
> turning back."

Dear Jesus,
I choose You today and every day! Fill me with Your strength. Fill me
with Your love. Help me, Lord, to . . .

Thank You

Dear Jesus,
Thank you, Lord, for this season. Thank you for opening my eyes to the things I need to change to be more like You. Please continue to walk with me as we draw near the cross. Thank you for loving me. Thank you for dying for me. Thank you for never giving up on me and calling me Your child. In Your blessed name, Amen.

Dear Jesus,
This month has been hard. It has been challenging to look this closely at myself and believe that You love me, despite my sin and the mistakes that I've made. But I can feel Your presence. I've heard Your gentle whisper. I see how You are preparing my heart. Thank you for this journey. Help me, Lord, keep going, as we move closer to the cross. Help me today . . .

April

TO THE CROSS

*"I have been crucified with Christ and I no longer
live, but Christ lives in me. The life I now live in the body,
I live by faith in the Son of God, who loved me
and gave himself for me."*

—GALATIANS 2:20

In the Beginning

*"In the beginning was the Word, and the Word was with
God, and the Word was God. He was with God in the
beginning. Through him all things were made; without him
nothing was made that has been made. In him was life,
and that life was the light of all mankind. The light shines
in the darkness, but the darkness has not overcome it."*
—JOHN 1:1–5

"In the beginning . . ." Do you remember your beginning? Maybe it was the beginning of your marriage and all the promises you held onto. Or the beginning of your family and your new role as a mom or dad. Maybe it was the beginning of illness or a season of life where all you experienced was loss. Beginnings can hold promise and pain, joy and sorrow.

But when God begins something, he will continue His work until it is finally finished. He started with Jesus, and it will end with Jesus. And to prove that, in the middle He built a cross. The cross represents the promise that if we believe that Jesus died for us to save us from our sins we will have eternal life. No matter our beginning, our end will be in heaven. Do you believe that? Maybe you need more time. This month we will be looking at this wonderful gift that Jesus gave to us. He came to earth to show us how to live and love one another, and He died in our place. Let's make our way to the cross . . .

Dear Jesus,
Thank you for the work You have started in me. Help me, Lord, as we
move toward the cross. Open my heart for everything You want to say.
Help me . . .

Burdens

"Come to me, all you who are weary and burdened, and I will give you rest. Take my yoke upon you and learn from me, for I am gentle and humble in heart, and you will find rest for your souls. For my yoke is easy and my burden is light."
—MATTHEW 11:28-30

What burdens do you have today? I know the feeling—carrying around a heavy heart and feeling the weight of my situation on my shoulders. It's exhausting and painful and you think no one will understand. But God does! He created us. He knows everything about us. He holds out His hand with an invitation into His rest. The best thing I ever did was take His hand and trust Him. I invite you today . . . call out to Him.

Below, write down your burdens. Give your situation, your pain, your loneliness, your burdens to the Lord. You will find rest for your soul.

Dear Jesus,
Today, I give You my burdens. I give You my . . .

Blessed

*Jesus said, "Blessed are the poor in spirit, for theirs is the
kingdom of heaven. Blessed are those who mourn, for they
will be comforted. Blessed are the meek, for they
will inherit the earth. Blessed are those who hunger and
thirst for righteousness, for they will be filled.
Blessed are the merciful, for they will be shown mercy.
Blessed are the pure in heart, for they will see God. Blessed
are the peacemakers, for they will be called children of God.
Blessed are those who are persecuted because
of righteousness, for theirs is the kingdom of heaven."*
—MATTHEW 5:3–10

*B*lessed. Have you ever thought that your trials could be a blessing? James writes in James 1:12, "Blessed is the one who perseveres under trial because, having stood the test, that person will receive the crown of life that the Lord has promised to those who love him."

I have had many trials, and I know that I am blessed. Knowing what I know now, and seeing how God has worked through my life, I wouldn't change the road I've walked. I wouldn't want to go back and bypass all of the pain and heartache I have endured. It has made me who I am today. I am blessed and count it all joy.

What blessings, including those that might at first glance seem opposing or negative, are you experiencing right now? What lessons are you learning about yourself?

Dear Jesus,
Thank you for this day. Thank you for these blessings. I am learning
through each one to . . .

The Death of Self

C. S. Lewis writes in *Mere Christianity*, "Repentance means unlearning all the self-conceit and self-will that we have been training ourselves into . . . It means killing part of yourself, undergoing a kind of death."

When I came into this realization, I knew that I would need to die to myself to be remade. I had so much sticking to me—so many things that I had added that I thought were important, and so many cracks and holes that needed to be repaired. However, this felt less like a pottery class and more like God picking me up, shaking off all the things that were sticking to me, and filling me with Himself. The process was painful . . . and necessary.

I had to unlearn all of the things I had been doing to make it through this life and learn to count on God for everything. And He walked with me, step by step, as I gave Him more and more of myself until I was alive in Him.

Is there something today that you need to put to death in yourself? Maybe it started as a small secret and now has taken over your life. Or maybe you have a habit that you haven't been able to break no matter how hard you try to let it go. Take these things to the cross. Pour them out to the Lord. Let them clink and clang noisily to the ground until the bag you've been carrying is empty and you are free. He will transform you into a new creation, and you will feel what it is to be alive in Him.

Dear Jesus,

Help me, Lord. I am not how You originally designed me to be. I have so much sticking to me, so many cracks and holes that need to be repaired. I pour them out to You today. All of the . . .

When We Look to the Cross

In the words of Chris Tomlinson, "Here's why the cross matters: It is at the cross that we see most clearly. If history were the vastness of space, the cross would be the brightest star. We see the fullness of God's being most clearly at the cross. We see the fullness of His active purposes most clearly at the cross."

It's when we look to the cross that we see God's:

Love

Restoration

Forgiveness

Wrath

Power

His love is why He sent Jesus to the cross, to restore all things to Himself. His forgiveness for our sins cancelled out the wrath that we are so deserving of. His power was shown to all by His raising Jesus from the dead. He changed everything, and He did it with a cross.

Father God,
Thank you for sending Your Son, Jesus. Thank you for forgiving me and making a way so that even I can have everlasting life. Jesus, please come into my heart. I invite You to live there. Please change me and teach me to be more like You. In Your name I pray these things. Amen.

Dear Jesus,
Thank you for this day. Help me, Lord, to look at Your cross. Help me to . . .

God's Temple

"Don't you know that you yourselves are God's temple and
that God's Spirit dwells in your midst?"
—1 CORINTHIANS 3:16

Do you believe that? Do you believe that you are God's temple? This is hard to believe, and even more so when we don't feel Him inside us. But how are you treating your temple? Is it filled with loud noises and violent images? Is it a spacious place of peace and rest or so full of boxes and old furniture that there is no place for God to live? Maybe it's time to clean house. Maybe it's time to put some things at the curb, open up the windows, and let the fresh breeze of the Holy Spirit fill you.

And how do you do that? Quiet your world, take time to rest, imagine that Jesus is walking with you every moment of the day. Would you sit with Jesus and watch certain movies or read certain books? Is He with you in every conversation that you're having? Make time each day to be in His Word, and listen for His voice. Before you know it, your house will be in order, and you will feel His presence in all that you do.

Dear Jesus,
Thank you for this day. Help me, Lord, to quiet my world and listen . . .

A Costly Offering

Have you ever given the Lord a costly offering? Mary of Bethany did. She poured out a year's worth of perfume on Jesus. And while her act seemed wasteful to others, Jesus received her offering with love.

> "'Leave her alone,' said Jesus. 'Why are you bothering her? She has done a beautiful thing to me. The poor you will always have with you, and you can help them any time you want. But you will not always have me. She did what she could. She poured perfume on my body beforehand to prepare me for my burial. Truly I tell you, wherever the gospel is preached throughout the world, what she has done will also be told, in memory of her.'"
> —MARK 14:6-9

Is there something you have to offer Jesus that will come at a great cost? Are you willing and ready to give it?

Dear Jesus,
Please forgive me for the times I have been unwilling to be uncomfortable.
Please forgive me for when I held on too tightly and wasn't willing to give You my costly offering. Today, I offer You . . .

Waiting

*"I wait for the L*ORD*, my whole being waits,*
and in his word I put my hope."
—PSALM 130:5

Waiting is hard. And it's easy to get ahead of ourselves and work on our own agenda while we're waiting for God. We're helping Him out, right? I've rationalized that before. But to truly wait for Him, wait for His next move, is so challenging . . . unless we put our hope and trust in His promises. Sometimes it's clinging to the very next thing He'll reveal to us. It's pulling His words and cradling them against our heart. And while we're waiting, He will speak to us. He will affirm our waiting and give us His rest and peace. But we need to wait. We need to trust. We need to be in His Word, listening.

I challenge you today that if there is something that God has asked you to wait on, stay true to His course. Wait. He knows that it's hard. But He will give you the strength. And it will be so worth it when the waiting is finally over.

Dear Jesus,
Thank you for this day. Help me, Lord, to wait for You and . . .

The Good News

"At daybreak, Jesus went out to a solitary place. The people were looking for him and when they came to where he was, they tried to keep him from leaving them. But he said, 'I must proclaim the good news of the kingdom of God to the other towns also, because that is why I was sent.' And he kept on preaching in the synagogues of Judea."

—LUKE 4:42-44

Do you know why Jesus was sent? The above verse tells us it was to preach the good news of the kingdom of God. I've read this over many times, but it never really sank in until our pastor spent a Sunday morning camped on this verse. I underlined it and made a note so that every time I read it I would not forget. Jesus came to preach the good news.

So my question for you today is: If we are called to be like Christ, then shouldn't we try to live in a way that exemplifies the reason Jesus was sent to us? Shouldn't we be telling everyone the good news about the kingdom of God before it's too late? I know the enemy doesn't want this. He will tell us every lie imaginable so that we feel we are not qualified or ready to share about our Lord or what's to come: "You're not a speaker!" "You don't like to confront people!" "You're so busy!" "What will you say?" "What if they have questions you can't answer?" But the truth is that we don't have to have all the answers. We can point them to the truth—the Bible. And we don't have to necessarily go out and tell people anything. All we have to do is love. Love the world as Jesus loved, and they will come to you.

Dear Jesus,
Thank you for this day. Help me, Lord, to share Your good news. Help me to . . .

Be Still and Know

This morning I opened my Bible. Not to the book-marked page in Chronicles; I needed to hear something specific from God. My heart was heavy from discussions with my husband, worry over my mom's illness, and wondering about life's next steps. I opened to Psalm 46, thankful to read that God is our refuge and strength. And then I come to the tenth verse: "Be still, and know that I am God." In my tiredness and confusion and sadness, I didn't realize I had opened to my life verse—the verse I have clung to all these years.

You, Lord, are an awesome God! Please forgive me for doubting. Please forgive me for not trusting. Please forgive me for not being still. I love you. me.

Dear Jesus,
Thank you for this day. Help me, Lord, to be still and know that You are God by . . .

Love Your Enemies

"But to you who are listening I say: Love your enemies, do good to those who hate you, bless those who curse you, pray for those who mistreat you. If someone slaps you on one cheek, turn to them the other also. If someone takes your coat, do not withhold your shirt from them. Give to everyone who asks you, and if anyone takes what belongs to you, do not demand it back. Do to others as you would have them do to you.

If you love those who love you, what credit is that to you? Even sinners love those who love them. And if you do good to those who are good to you, what credit is that to you? Even sinners do that. And if you lend to those from whom you expect repayment, what credit is that to you? Even sinners lend to sinners, expecting to be repaid in full. But love your enemies, do good to them, and lend to them without expecting to get anything back. Then your reward will be great, and you will be children of the Most High, because he is kind to the ungrateful and wicked. Be merciful, just as your Father is merciful."

—LUKE 6:27-36

Dear Jesus,
Thank you for Your Word. Help me, Lord, to love my enemies. Help me to . . .

Sowing Seed

"While a large crowd was gathering and people were coming to Jesus from town after town, he told this parable: 'A farmer went out to sow his seed. As he was scattering the seed some fell along the path; it was trampled on, and the birds ate it up. Some fell on rocky ground, and when it came up, the plants withered because they had no moisture. Other seed fell among thorns, which grew up with it and choked the plants. Still other seed fell on good soil. It came up and yielded a crop, a hundred times more than was sown.' . . .

His disciples asked him what the parable meant. He said, . . .

'This is the meaning of the parable: The seed is the word of God. Those along the path are the ones who hear, and then the devil comes and takes away the word from their hearts, so that they may not believe and be saved. Those on the rocky ground are the ones who receive the word with joy when they hear it, but they have no root. They believe for a while, but in the time of testing they fall away. The seed that fell among thorns stands for those who hear, but as they go on their way they are choked by life's worries, riches and pleasures, and they do not mature. But the seed on good soil stands for those with a noble and good heart, who hear the word, retain it, and by persevering produce a crop.'"

—LUKE 8:4–15

Dear Jesus,
Thank you for this day. Help me, Lord, to plant Your Word in my heart
so that . . .

Faith in the Storm

"One day Jesus said to his disciples, 'Let's go over to the other side of the lake.' So, they got into a boat and set out. As they sailed, he fell asleep. A squall came down on the lake, so that the boat was being swamped, and they were in great danger.

The disciples went and woke him, saying, 'Master, Master, we're going to drown!'

He got up and rebuked the wind and the raging waters; the storm subsided, and all was calm. 'Where is your faith?' he asked his disciples.

In fear and amazement they asked one another, 'Who is this? He commands even the winds and the water, and they obey him.'"

—LUKE 8:22–25

Dear Lord,
Forgive me for not trusting You in the storm. Help me to have faith and know that You command the wind and the waves and that You will protect me in all things. In Jesus' name, Amen.

Dear Jesus,
Thank you for this day. Help me, Lord, to demonstrate my faith in You by . . .

Detours

As Billy Graham points out, "The cross is offensive because it confronts people. Even so, it's a confrontation that all of us must face. There is no other way of salvation except through the cross of Christ."

You know the experience of trying to get from Point A to Point B when there's a detour. You follow the orange signs, arrows that turn you left and then right, and before long you've come out on the other side of the construction zone and you're back on your way. I think a problem we face is that much of life is filled with detours. We go off course, winding our way around until we get back on the right road, and this happens day in and day out. When it comes to salvation, it's hard to believe that there is only one way to get there—through Jesus.

But people still stop and ask for directions: Are your sure it's not through hard work? Are you positive that I can't get there because I'm a good person? What about my money . . . I have a lot of money . . . Can't I buy my way there?

But the answer to all three is no. And aren't you secretly glad? The greatest gift that was ever given is free to anyone and everyone; there's just one way to get there . . . through the cross of Christ. Amen!

Dear Jesus,
Thank you for this day. Help me, Lord, to not get hung up in a detour.
Help me to stay on Your path by . . .

The One

"Now the tax collectors and sinners were all gathering around to hear Jesus. But the Pharisees and the teachers of the law muttered, 'This man welcomes sinners and eats with them.'

Then Jesus told them this parable: 'Suppose one of you has a hundred sheep and loses one of them. Doesn't he leave the ninety-nine in the open country and go after the lost sheep until he finds it? And when he finds it, he joyfully puts it on his shoulders and goes home. Then he calls his friends and neighbors together and says, "Rejoice with me; I have found my lost sheep." I tell you that in the same way there will be more rejoicing in heaven over one sinner who repents than over ninety-nine righteous persons who do not need to repent.'"

—LUKE 15:1–7

Dear Jesus,
Thank you that You chase after me—that when I go astray You find me
and save me. Help me to . . .

The Cross of Christ

W hat does the cross of Christ mean to you? Oswald Chambers writes, "The cross of Christ is the revealed truth of God's judgement on sin. Never associate the idea of martyrdom with the cross of Christ. It was the supreme triumph, and it shook the very foundations of hell. There is nothing in time or eternity more absolutely certain and irrefutable than what Jesus accomplished on the cross. He made it possible for the entire human race to be brought back into a right-standing relationship with God. He made redemption the foundation of human life; that is, He made a way for every person to have fellowship with God."

Dear Jesus,

Thank you for everything You accomplished on the cross. Thank you for . . .

Stand Firm

"Some of his disciples were remarking about how the temple was adorned with beautiful stones and with gifts dedicated to God. But Jesus said, 'As for what you see here, the time will come when not one stone will be left on another; every one of them will be thrown down.'

'Teacher,' they asked, 'when will these things happen? And what will be the sign that they are about to take place?'

He replied: 'Watch out that you are not deceived. For many will come in my name, claiming, "I am he," and "The time is near." Do not follow them. When you hear of wars and revolutions, do not be frightened. These things must happen first, but the end will not come right away. . . .

But before all this, they will seize you and persecute you. They will hand you over to synagogues and put you in prison, and you will be brought before kings and governors, and all on account of my name. And so you will bear testimony to me. But make up your mind not to worry beforehand how you will defend yourselves. For I will give you words and wisdom that none of your adversaries will be able to resist or contradict. You will be betrayed even by parents, brothers and sisters, relatives and friends, and they will put some of you to death. Everyone will hate you because of me. But not a hair on your head will perish. Stand firm, and you will win life.'"

—LUKE 21:5–9, 12–15

Dear Jesus,

There is so much happening in this world that makes me question, "Is the end near?" Help me, Lord, when I am afraid. Help me to hear Your truth amongst all the lies. Help me to stand firm on Your promises. Help me to . . .

The Last Supper

"When the hour came, Jesus and his apostles reclined at the table. And he said to them, 'I have eagerly desired to eat this Passover with you before I suffer. For I tell you, I will not eat it again until it finds fulfillment in the kingdom of God.'

After taking the cup, he gave thanks and said, 'Take this and divide it among you. For I tell you I will not drink again of the fruit of the vine until the kingdom of God comes.'

And he took the bread, gave thanks and broke it, and gave it to them, saying, 'This is my body given for you; do this in remembrance of me.'

In the same way, after the supper he took the cup, saying, 'This cup is the new covenant in my blood, which is poured out for you. But the hand of him who is going to betray me is with mine on the table. The Son of Man will go as it has been decreed, but woe to that man who betrays him!'"

—LUKE 22:14-22

When they were finished with the supper, they sung a hymn and went out to the Mount of Olives, and then on to Gethsemane. There Jesus prayed: "'Abba, Father,' he said, 'everything is possible for you. Take this cup from me, yet not what I will, but what you will.'"

—MARK 14:36

Later, he was taken and arrested and brought before the Sanhedrin.

Dear Jesus,

Thank you for this day. Thank you for communion. Thank you that You've given us a way to remember what You did for us. Thank you for . . .

The Cup of Wrath

My Lord, my God, how You suffered for me! You were spit on and mocked and beaten until You were barely recognizable. You were nailed to a cross by your hands and feet and wore a crown of thorns. And on top of all that, You bore the weight of the sin of all humankind—past, present and future. You drank God's cup of wrath so that we could be set free. I cry out to You today and say thank you, although those words taste awful in my mouth. There are no words that can express my gratefulness and love. Please look into my heart, see the brokenness I feel, and help me to be more like You, every day of my life.

> "At noon, darkness came over the whole land until three in the afternoon. And at three in the afternoon Jesus cried out in a loud voice, 'Eloi, Eloi, lema sabacthani?' (which means 'My God, my God, why have you forsaken me?').
>
> When some of those standing near heard this, they said, 'Listen, he's calling Elijah.'
>
> Someone ran, filled a sponge with wine vinegar, put it on a staff, and offered it to Jesus to drink. 'Now leave him alone. Let's see if Elijah comes to take him down,' he said.
>
> With a loud cry, Jesus breathed his last.
>
> The curtain of the temple was torn in two from top to bottom. And when the centurion, who stood there in front of Jesus, saw how he died, he said, 'Surely this man was the Son of God!'"
> —MARK 15:33–39

Dear Jesus,
Thank you for this day. Thank you for dying on the cross, for it was my
sin that held You there. Thank you for . . .

Waiting

And so we wait. We wait for the morning when the stone will be rolled away. We wait for the moment when we will hear, "'Don't be alarmed . . . You are looking for Jesus the Nazarene, who was crucified. He has risen! He is not here." (Mark 16:6).

But today we sit in silence. We sit in the uncomfortable. We sit in the waiting, which is always hard to do. We remember what yesterday was and how we have been changed forever. Today the heavens and earth are quiet, but we wait for tomorrow when the whole world will sing! Amen!

Dear Jesus,

Thank you for this day. Help me, Lord, to wait in the silence. Help me to . . .

He Is Risen!

Hallelujah! Let us rejoice to the world that our Lord is alive! He has overcome the grave and we are free! Free from pain, free from death, free from sins. Praise His holy name!

"When the Sabbath was over, Mary Magdalene, Mary the mother of James, and Salome bought spices so they might go to anoint Jesus' body. Very early on the first day of the week, just after sunrise, they were on their way to the tomb and they asked each other, 'Who will roll the stone away from the entrance of the tomb?'

But when they looked up, they saw that the stone, which was very large, had been rolled away. As they entered the tomb, they saw a young man dressed in a white robe sitting on the right side, and they were alarmed.

'Don't be alarmed,' he said. 'You are looking for Jesus the Nazarene, who was crucified. He has risen! He is not here. See the place where they laid him. But go, tell his disciples and Peter, "He is going ahead of you into Galilee. There you will see him, just as he told you."'

—MARK 16:1–7

Dear Jesus,

You are the name above all names! I worship You today! You have conquered death and with that have given me everlasting life! I love you, Lord! I praise Your holy name! My heart declares that . . .

Washed Clean

For years I was blinded by the enemy's lies. When I accepted the truth and Jesus' love, my eyes were finally opened. It was as though scales had fallen off and I could see. Everything I had been searching for had been in front of me the whole time. I could not only see the truth but feel it all around me.

> "And you also were included in Christ when you heard the message of truth, the gospel of your salvation. When you believed, you were marked in him with a seal, the promised Holy Spirit, who is a deposit guaranteeing our inheritance until the redemption of those who are God's possession—to the praise of his glory."
> —EPHESIANS 1:13–15

At that moment I knew what I had to do. Our church was making announcements for the upcoming baptism that would be held that year on Easter Sunday. It was as though a light bulb went off. I wanted to get baptized. I had been baptized as a young girl but felt a lifetime of sin clinging to my frame. I wanted to unite myself with Jesus once again. I wanted to wash away my old self and bind myself to Him on the anniversary of that day when so long ago He bound Himself to us.

So, on April 20, 2014, I stepped into the pool of water. I claimed His forgiveness for my sins and dipped back underneath the cool water. My chains were broken and my stains cleaned. I came up alive and brand new and took in my first breath as the daughter of the mighty King, ready to follow Him wherever He would lead.

Dear Jesus,
I'm listening. Lord. Speak to my heart today. Help me to . . .

The Battle Is Real

The battle is real, my friends. Easter Sunday is joyous and full of celebration, but the days afterward can be like fighting tooth and nail against the enemy! Arm yourselves! Put on the breastplate of righteousness, the shoes of the gospel, the shield of faith, the helmet of salvation, and the sword of the Spirit. Rebuke the enemy and his lies and whispers of discouragement. Do not give up! Do not grow weary!

> "For our struggle is not against flesh and blood, but against the rulers, against the authorities, against the powers of this dark world and against the spiritual forces of evil in the heavenly realms."
> —EPHESIANS 6:12

Dear Jesus,
I pray for my friend who is reading this today! Guard her with Your angels and protect her from evil. Put a hedge of protection around his home and family. Equip them for the battle today. They can do all things through You, who strengthens them. In Your name I pray, Amen.

Dear Jesus,
Guard me with Your angels and protect me from the evil one. Help me, Lord, to . . .

Find the Joy

It's easy to get caught up in all the negative things going on in this world. After a long day at school or work or taking care of your children or grandchildren, watching sixty minutes of your local and world news can solidify all the negative things you felt throughout the day. Are we fighting a losing battle? Maybe, just maybe, we are focusing on the wrong things. What if today you praised Him? What if you praised Jesus for His love for you? Praised Him for the breath in your lungs, or for your job or for the food in your fridge. Praised Him for the hugs from your children or for the birds singing right outside your window. Find the joy. Accept the love. Accept the truth that no matter what is going on in our world nothing can separate us from God's love.

> "For I am convinced that neither death not life, neither angels nor demons, neither the present nor the future, nor any powers, neither height nor depth, nor anything else in all creation, will be able to separate us from the love of God that is in Christ Jesus our Lord."
> —ROMANS 8:38–39

Dear Jesus,
Thank you for this day. I praise You for who You are! Help me to be
strong in You so I can . . .

Seventy-Seven Times

D o you ever wonder how many times you should forgive someone? Peter asked Jesus if it was seven times, but Jesus said it was seventy-seven times (Matthew 18:22)—meaning as many times as it takes. Do you have someone you still need to forgive? Are you holding onto the bitterness and anger that go along with unforgiveness? If so, you are only hurting yourself and your relationship with God. We need to remember that Christ died to forgive *all* our sins, not just some of them. Let us try to pass that forgiveness on to others.

> "Be kind and compassionate to one another, forgiving each other,
> just as in Christ God forgave you."
> —EPHESIANS 4:32

Dear Jesus,
Thank you that You died for all of my sins—past, present, and future.
Help me to remember that when I need to forgive someone. Help me,
Lord, to forgive . . .

Eternity

Are you living for today? I did once, making choices that felt good, not caring what tomorrow would bring. I said what I wanted without realizing the consequences or caring about the feelings of the other person. I thought only about myself and my survival and was wrapped up in my own self-pity and depression. I didn't see the gift that we are given each day when we open our eyes—or, more importantly, that this life won't be over when we someday close our eyes. We have an eternity with Jesus—if we choose. Or we can have an eternity without Him . . .

What will you choose today? I would urge you to choose Jesus. It's the best choice I've ever made.

> "Jesus said to her, 'I am the resurrection and the life. He who believes in me will live, even though they die; and whoever lives by believing in me will never die.'"
> —JOHN 11:25-26

Dear Jesus,
Help me to remember that the choices I make today effect my eternity.
I choose You. Lord! Help me to walk in Your truth and see the many
gifts You give. Help me to . . .

The Next Step

In 2015 I had the opportunity to go to Guatemala with my husband and a group from our church and build houses. While the experience was amazing and I loved that I could give back and function as the hands and feet of Jesus, I had no idea how God would work in my heart. It was in our morning devotions each day, in the moments of worship and reflection, that God asked me the question. Some of the lessons I had written down in my journal were from different speakers and different days, but in the end they all asked the same thing: Was I ready to take the next step? These were some of the things I wrote down:

- Come humbly.
- Pray according to God's will.
- Come to God with repentance.
- Stop sinning and turn away from sin.
- Come willing to ask.
- Come willing to submit.
- Have an attitude and heart of praise.
- Do I want to be a Christian robot?
- Where is the growth with this routine?
- Am I bearing fruit?
- God wants us to experience new things and a deeper relationship with Him.

What is God saying to you right now? Are you listening?

Dear Jesus,
Thank you for this day. Help me, Lord, to . . .

The Road

We have all had tests in our life. We have all walked dark roads, felt as though we were trapped beneath the earth, and scaled treacherous hills to climb up out of our situations. But ultimately, we are defined not by the things that will eventually come our way but how we walk through those situations and come out the other side. Never forget that Jesus walked a road that ended at a cross, but He overcame so that we might have everlasting life.

I know one thing: I would not be who I am today if not for the many challenges I've faced. I count it all joy that God has walked with me, changed me, and made me a new creation. Today, can you see the joy?

> "Consider it pure joy, my brothers and sisters, whenever you face trials of many kinds, because you know that the testing of your faith produces perseverance."
> —JAMES 1:2–3

Dear Jesus,
Thank you for this day. Thank you for the road that I've walked. Help me to find the joy in this journey and to . . .

I See You

"Do you know that I see you? I see you at school and the workplace. I see you when you're home at night. I know when you've had a hard day or when you're struggling with something. I feel every bit of pain, every disappointment, every fear. I need you to know that I've walked this earth and felt what you've felt. You may not understand why I did what I did on the cross, but I did it for you. If you'll let me, I'll carry what you're hanging onto and give you the strength for your journey. I'll give you peace in this world of chaos and confusion and love you for who you are, because I created you. Will you let me?"—Jesus

Dear Jesus,
Thank you for this day. Thank you for loving me. Thank you for . . .

To Be More Like Him

I know this has been a challenging two months. We've looked into the deepest part of our souls and repented over our sin. We've walked where Jesus walked and watched His life unfold. We traveled to the cross and watched our Savior die before our very eyes, and we watched Him rise again. But in doing all of these things, I hope we've learned more about ourselves and what it's like to have Jesus live in us.

Traveling to the cross is not an easy journey, but it's a necessary one if we want to be more like Him. We need to tear down the walls we build around ourselves and allow the Holy Spirit to breathe into us truth and love and equip us with what we need to take to the world. Are you ready?

Dear Jesus,

Thank you for this journey to the cross! Thank you for what You've showed me and what I've learned. Fill me with the Holy Spirit. Help me, Lord, to be more like You. Help me . . .

May

A MONTH OF LETTING GO . . .

"Jabez cried out to the God of Israel,
'Oh, that you would bless me
and enlarge my territory!
Let your hand be with me,
and keep me from harm so that
I will be free from pain.'"

−1 CHRONICLES 4:10

The Act of Letting Go

Before we walk through all of the things we would like to let go of, we need to start with the basics: How do we do it? The hardest thing about letting go is the act itself. We are opening up our clenched hands and lifting our palms to the sky, saying "God, I can't carry this anymore." Throughout the next 31 days, practice this exercise every time you are tempted to take something back—even if it's several times a day. To live a surrendered life, the only thing we need to hold onto is God Himself.

We also need to be open to all of the things God wants us to let go of and do in our life. The prayer of Jabez was a prayer I prayed diligently when I was learning to let go and live for Him: "Oh that you would bless me and enlarge my territory! Let your hand be with me, and keep me from harm so that I will be free from pain" (1 Chronicles 4:10). The prayer isn't about letting go but about living expectantly and trusting God with our lives.

I look forward to seeing what God will show you over the next 31 days as we make this journey together.

Dear Jesus,
Thank you for this day. Help me to be open and prepare my heart to let go of . . .

Letting Go and Switching Focus

I know that for me, when I was going through my divorce, it was challenging not to be thinking about myself and how awful I felt all the time. It wasn't until I started to switch my focus from myself to how I could help other people that my perception of my situation changed and I felt better. I volunteered at a shelter doing dishes and became more active in my kids' youth group. I realized I wasn't the only one in the world hurting, and when my eyes were opened and I switched my focus it was easier to let go of my own pain.

If you're at this point right now and you need to get out of your own head and start moving on and letting go, try volunteering or helping someone else. When you switch your focus from yourself, you're giving God the chance to move and work in you and through you. When you do this, you're on the right path to letting go.

> "Trust in the LORD with all your heart
> and lean not on your own understanding;
> in all your ways submit to him,
> and he will make your paths straight."
> —PROVERBS 3:5-6

Dear Jesus,

Thank you for this day. Help me to be open and switch my focus to . . .

Letting Go and Finding You

How many of us at one time or another have found our identity in someone or something else? I know I have. I went to this person for everything. I even saw myself and my value through his eyes. But when things changed and we grew apart, what I saw in his eyes changed the way I felt about myself, and I almost disappeared. When the relationship was over, I poured myself into my job. My value became tied up in how well I succeeded at work and the praise I received from others.

It wasn't until God showed me that my value is in Him that I could put my job in its proper perspective. I could also then love someone else without losing myself. How did I do it? I had to stop believing the lies from the enemy that I had no value. I had to let go of everything that I had ever believed about myself and replace the lies with the truth. God loves me. I am His. He died for me, even while I was a sinner. He wants to be my everything. And He wants you to believe all of these things too. Let go of what you once believed about yourself. Let go and you will find you.

> "Praise be to the God and Father of our Lord Jesus Christ! In his great mercy he has given us new birth into a living hope through the resurrection of Jesus Christ from the dead."
> —1 PETER 1:3

Dear Jesus,
Thank you for this day. Help me to find my value in You and . . .

Letting Go of Control

Okay, a show of hands . . . How many of you like to be in control? I know I used to "need" to be, but not as much anymore, and I think there is a definite difference between "like" and "need." When things were going on around me that I couldn't control, I would feel a need to manipulate things in my life to give me the illusion of control. Like furniture—I used to move furniture around sometimes twice a week. If I couldn't control my situation, I would control my surroundings.

What about you? Are there things in your life that you feel a need to be in control of? If so, make a list, so you can name the issues and address them one by one. Take each one before God in prayer and ask Him to reveal to you why you feel the need for control. The path of letting go is admitting that there is something you are hanging onto, addressing it, and giving it to God. Open your clenched fist and remember that God is in control and that He's got this, no matter how big or small.

> "I am the LORD, the God of all mankind. Is anything too hard for me?"
> —JEREMIAH 32:27

Dear Jesus,
Thank you for this day. Help me to name what I "need" control of, and help me let go of . . .

Letting Go of the Past

We all have a past. We all have experiences we have gone through that have somehow shaped us or perhaps define who we are today. Deciding whether or not you need to let go of your past is determining how much of your past is in your present.

When I got remarried, it was blatantly obvious that I was hanging onto the past and still carrying all of the baggage from my youth. I reacted to situations as if I were still married to my first husband and started growing a garden of bitterness and resentment that I watered daily. Even though these were different men and different marriages, I was stuck in the past and saw no hope of going back to the person I once was, only sinking further and further into a hole of regret.

It wasn't until I was invited to experience a day of prayer and confronted my past head on that I was able to let go and move on. I prayed and confessed over every hurt, every mistake, every lie until I was free and able to leave my baggage at the cross. I walked in carrying luggage for a yearlong trip and walked out carrying only my purse.

While God is in our past, present, and future, He tell us in Isaiah 43:18–19, "Forget the former things; do not dwell on the past. See, I am doing a new thing! Now it springs up; do you not perceive it?"

To focus on our past is to miss out on what God is doing for us today. I'm praying today that you can bring before the Lord your past with thanksgiving, and ask Him to help you live in the present with joy! Amen.

Dear Jesus,

Thank you for this day. Help me to let go of the past and let go of . . .

Letting Go of People Pleasing

I am a people pleaser. I like people to be happy, and I hate the thought of someone being unhappy with me. I used to go out of my way to make sure I hadn't disappointed someone by my words or actions and that I was doing everything I could to please them. Do you know how exhausting this is? Maybe you do because you are a people pleaser too.

But one day the Lord revealed to me that I have no control over how another person interprets my actions or words. Maybe they are having a bad day. Maybe they are going through something right now that is devastating, and nothing I can do or say will make them happy. I can only live to please God and have my actions glorify Him.

When I accepted this as truth, it was freeing to let it go. I needed only to please God. If I centered my actions around pleasing Him and doing what is right in His eyes, then the rest would take care of itself.

Are you a people pleaser, focusing more on what others think about you than what God does? Trust the words of Colossians 3:23–24: "Whatever you do, work at it with all your heart, as working for the Lord, not for human masters, since you know that you will receive an inheritance from the Lord as a reward. It is the Lord Christ you are serving."

Dear Jesus,
Thank you for this day. Help me to let go of people pleasing and to focus on pleasing You. Help me to . . .

Letting Go of Comparing Yourself to Others

There is a reason the saying "The grass in always greener on the other side" has been around for ages. It is very challenging not to look at someone else and say, *They have it all together, so why don't I?* But the truth is that we don't walk in their shoes. When we compare ourselves to other people, we are seeing only what they are choosing to show us, and it's easy to show people only what you want them to see. I should know, because I did that for years. I hid from everyone that I was drowning in an illness, in our bankruptcy, and in our troubled marriage. But while you're trying to let everyone believe that you're okay and have it all together, it's a lie. It's exhausting and unhealthy, and not what God wants for our lives.

God made each of us different, with different strengths and different abilities. We need to celebrate and be thankful for what we have and not get caught up in the lie that the grass is greener somewhere else. If we do this, we can let go and live as God intended.

> "Each one must test their own actions. Then they can take pride in themselves alone, without comparing themselves to someone else, for each one should carry their own load."
> —GALATIANS 6:4–5

Dear Jesus,
Thank you for this day. Help me to let go of comparing myself to others and to be thankful for what You are doing in my life. Help me to . . .

Letting Go of Regret

I love pancakes and maple syrup. I love the smell and taste and how they start to instantly make my hunger go away. But then they start to expand and fill in all the crevices of my stomach, and I can't get the maple syrup off my fingers. It's sticky and messy, and when I'm done I'm stuffed and want to take a nap. I think regret is very similar to eating pancakes. We have good intentions, but before we know it an action has taken on a life of its own.

While it might have seemed like a good idea at the time, now it's too late and we can't easily fix it—we just have to wait it out. There's a sticky residue that stays with us, and it's hard to wash off. All we would like to do is cover our heads and wait for it to be over.

I have things I have regretted in my life. And I remember the feeling I had before I gave that regret to Jesus Christ. Regret had taken up residence and started to eat away at who I was. I physically hurt and could no longer escape the pain.

But there is good news! We have hope in Jesus Christ. Just as Paul did when he wrote these words in prison: "Brothers and sisters, I do not consider myself yet to have taken hold of it. But one thing I do: Forgetting what is behind me and straining toward what is ahead, I press on toward the goal to win the prize for which God has called me heavenward in Christ Jesus" (Philippians 3:13–14).

Open up your clenched hand and give God all of the regret you are holding onto. Today is a new day, and it is sweet!

Dear Jesus,

Thank you for this day. Help me to let go of regret. Help me to . . .

Letting Go of Fear

No matter where you turn today, there is something you could be afraid of. The news is filled with bombings, shootings, bad weather, political unrest, . . . and the list goes on and on. And then there are the unknowns—financial, health, family, and our future. So how do we live without fear? Jesus says in John 14:27, "'Peace I leave you; my peace I give you. I do not give to you as the world gives. Do not let your hearts be troubled and do not be afraid.'"

To live without fear, we need to let go of the fear itself and hold onto His peace. So today, ask yourself *What am I afraid of?* Name it out loud and cover it by the blood of Jesus. The enemy wants us to be afraid because that limits us in how we live our lives. It limits us on how we can live for Jesus.

Some days you might need to pray over and over to be brave. But we need to remember that He is faithful and answers our prayers. "I sought the LORD, and he answered me; he delivered me from all my fears" (Psalm 34:4).

Dear Jesus,
Thank you for this day. Help me to let go of fear. Help me to . . .

Letting Go of Shame

Before we can let go of something, we need to name it and define it. Dr. James O'Henman says that shame "is a destructive, condemning judgment about self. It is a feeling and perception of self-rejection and self-hatred. Shame says, 'I am bad and wrong.' 'It's just who I am.' 'I am a mistake.' 'I am a failure.' Shame is a statement of identity rather than a statement about specific actions."

For years I carried shame. My mental illness defined who I was, and I hated myself. The enemy (the devil) poured lies on me, and I believed every one. It wasn't until I was so full of shame, regret, and bitterness that I agreed to a day of prayer. God walked me through every area of my life, replacing the lies with truth, and I was free. You see, I wasn't a mistake . . . and neither are you. We are God's creations. Sons and daughters of the King!

For more information on the lies we believe and how to pray into each one, head to my website and download "The ABC's of Salvation." It is a wonderful tool, filled with verses and statements of truth. I'm praying you believe this today!

Dear Jesus,
Thank you for this day. Help me to let go of shame. Help me to . . .

Letting Go of Pride

I've had many different levels of pride in my life. I had pride in my high school and our sports teams. I've had pride in my jobs and the work I've done. And I've had pride in my children and how they were growing up. I think these are wonderful things to have pride in and are healthy representations. But I've also had so much pride that I wasn't able to ask for help. So much pride that I thought I was too good to shop at certain stores. So much pride that I've treated people as though they were at a lower level than myself.

What about you? Do you have areas in your life where you struggle with pride? Is it more than being proud of your school or your work or your family?

Paul says in Romans 12:3, "For by the grace given me I say to every one of you: Do not think of yourself more highly than you ought, but rather think of yourself with sober judgment, in accordance with the faith God has distributed to each of you."

Help each of us, Lord, to "do nothing out of selfish ambition or vain conceit. Rather, in humility value others above yourself" (Philippians 2:3).

Dear Jesus,

Thank you for this day. Help me to let go of pride. Help me to . . .

Letting Go and Forgiving

*"Then Peter came to Jesus and asked, 'Lord, how
many times shall I forgive my brother or sister who sins
against me? Up to seven times?'"*
—MATTHEW 18:21-22

How about you, my friends? Are you having trouble forgiving someone, maybe even one time? The Bible is filled with powerful verses on forgiveness, as though God knew how hard this would be for us to do in our own strength. But we need to remember that Christ died for us while we were yet sinners.

It wasn't until I read this verse that I felt the full weight of how important forgiving others is to my own forgiveness. "'Do not judge, and you will not be judged. Do not condemn, and you will not be condemned. Forgive, and you will be forgiven,'" said Jesus (Luke 6:37).

We are not perfect. We sin and make mistakes every day. And so do other people.

We need to let go and forgive others as we want Jesus to forgive us. As we need Him to forgive us. Understanding this makes it easier to let go and forgive, and to love others as Jesus loves us.

Lord Jesus,
Help me to forgive others and love others as You love me. Thank you for this ultimate blessing!

Dear Jesus,
Thank you for this day. Help me to let go and forgive. Help me to . . .

Letting Go of Idols

What is an idol? Its definition is an image or representation of a god used as an object of worship. But to take that one step further, I think it's something we put before God and value or count on more than we do God Himself.

Money has always been used as an example. We spend our whole lives going after it—making it, spending it, worrying about it, loving it. Do we trust in money and believe it will take care of us, more so than we believe God will? Is it because we can touch it and see it and know we can use it for what we need? But I challenge you because I've seen God do those exact same things. I've had many idols in my life, but letting go of them and putting God above all else was the best thing I ever did, and I continue to keep in check my impulse to do otherwise.

Open up your clenched fist and let go of whatever you are holding onto tighter than you are to God. Once you do, you will find freedom in trusting that He will be enough.

> "The idols of the nations are silver and gold,
>> made by human hands.
> They have mouths, but cannot speak,
>> eyes, but cannot see.
> They have ears, but cannot hear,
>> nor is there breath in their mouths.
> Those who make them will be like them,
>> and so will all who trust in them"
> —PSALM 135:15–18

Dear Jesus,
Thank you for this day. Help me to let go of any idols I am holding onto.
Help me to . . .

Letting Go of Overthinking

One of the symptoms of bipolar disorder is racing thoughts. My mind used to race all the time with thoughts I couldn't control. But when it wasn't racing, I was overthinking. I would analyze everything and figure out every angle. There might be some situations where this isn't a bad thing, but I was doing this all the time, and it left no room for God's peace or for me to listen to His still, quiet voice. During this time God gave me a verse to hold onto. I would say this verse out loud to quiet my inner self and let His peace wash over me: "'Be still, and know that I am God'" (Psalm 46:10).

It wasn't just about being still; it was being reminded that God is in control. I can spend time overthinking, or I can trust God and the plans He has for my life. What about you? Will you trust Him today?

Dear Jesus,
Thank you for this day. Help me to let go of overthinking. Help me to . . .

Letting Go of Discouragement

It's easy to get discouraged, especially when we focus on the wrong things. When I watch the news, focus on what is going on in my own life, think about how busy work is, worry about the finances, worry about my children or my parents—and the list goes on and on . . . I can easily become discouraged. But if I switch my focus to God and trust Him to give me enough strength for whatever is directly in front of me at that moment, I can get through anything with His help.

It is my prayer that today you will let go of discouragement each time it creeps in and trust that God will walk with you, holding your hand. He will give you exactly what you need when you need it.

> "'Have I not commanded you? Be strong and courageous. Do not be afraid; do not be discouraged, for the LORD your God will be with you wherever you go.'"
> —JOSHUA 1:9

Dear Jesus,
Thank you for this day. Help me to let go discouragement. Help me to . . .

Letting Go of Disappointment

Disappointment comes in many forms. We can be disappointed when our favorite team loses or our favorite show is taken off the air. We can be disappointed over report cards and car door dents and rainy days when we were scheduled to go to the beach. We can be disappointed over job loss, loss of a friend, or when the person we trusted the most walks out of our life. Disappointment comes when an expectation doesn't get met or when something we wanted doesn't come true. The only way to let go of our disappointments is to give them to God. You need to trust that He has a plan for your life and sees what you need and what you don't.

In the words of an anonymous quote, "He knows the end from the beginning while we see just a short part of now."

> "Trust in the LORD with all your heart
> and lean not on your own understanding;
> in all your ways submit to him,
> and he will make your paths straight."
> —PROVERBS 3:5-6

Dear Jesus,
Thank you for this day. Help me to let go of disappointment. Help me to . . .

Letting Go of Anger

There are several verses in the Bible about anger. Ephesians 4:26–27 says, "In your anger do not sin. Do not let the sun go down while you are still angry." And James 1:20 says that "human anger does not produce the righteousness that God desires."

Proverbs 15:1 says, "A gentle answer turns away wrath, but a harsh word stirs up anger." And Jesus said in Matthew 5:22, "I tell you that anyone who is angry with a brother or sister will be subject to judgment. Again, anyone who says to a brother or sister "*Raca*" is answerable to the court. Anyone who says, "You fool!" will be in danger of the fire of hell.""

While anger is a human emotion, it's one we should not hold onto or let control us. Like everything else, we need to open up our clenched fist and give it to God. When we do this, He will give us the ability to forgive and let it go.

Dear Jesus,

Thank you for this day. Help me to let go of anger. Help me to . . .

Letting Go of Depression

I battled with depression for years. The lows were so low for a while that I didn't want to get out of bed, do the dishes, or clean the house. I didn't want to do anything. Some days I didn't even want to live. Speaking as someone who knows, depression is not something you want to keep to yourself. You need to reach out and speak up.

If it's medication you need for a while, or counseling—taking the first step is the hardest, but it will help. While I did both, I wasn't fully free until I gave it to God. For the longest time I didn't believe He could heal me . . . maybe He didn't *want* to heal me. But that was a lie from the enemy. Satan has come to steal and destroy, and there is no place else he would like you to be than at home, depressed, wanting to die.

Letting go of depression is admitting that you need help, taking the proper course of treatment, and letting God in to heal you. Take it from me—I am living proof.

Dear Jesus,

Thank you for this day. Help me to let go depression. Help me to . . .

Letting Go of Brokenness

Our world looks at brokenness as a weakness. If something is broken, it no longer has value and can be thrown out. But God looks at brokenness as an opportunity. When we let down our pride and independence and admit that we are broken, that we are nothing without God, we make room for God to rush in and resculpt us. We become a new creation. We become His original design, the way He intended us to be.

The day I stood in my kitchen and cried out to the Lord, "Lord, I give up. I'll do whatever you ask. But I can't do this on my own anymore," I was admitting that I was broken. But to truly be what God had created me to be, I understood that I would need to be resculpted. I had so much sticking to me, so many things I had added that I thought were important, and so many cracks and holes that needed to be repaired. I would need to be remade. However, this felt less like a pottery class and more like God picking me up, shaking off all of those things that were sticking to me, and filling me with Himself. The process was painful . . . and necessary. But God knew exactly what He was doing.

If you're ready to let go of your brokenness, cry out to the Lord. Lift your hands and let go . . . and let God. And get ready for something amazing!

Dear Jesus,

Thank you for this day. Help me to let go of my brokenness. Help me to . . .

Letting Go of Past Relationships

It's hard to say goodbye. Whether we do it by choice or it is out of our control, the pain can stay with us a long time. The only way to let go of past relationships is to pray. Pray every time you miss those people. Pray every time you are looking back. Pray every time your heart aches for them. God hears our prayers, quiets our hearts, and gives us hope. Hope for healing. Hope for peace.

> "May the God of hope fill you with all joy and peace as you trust in him, so that you may overflow with hope by the power of the Holy Spirit."
> —ROMANS 15:13

Dear Jesus,

Thank you for this day. Help me to let go of my past relationship. Help me to . . .

Letting Go of Hate

There are lots of things to "hate" in this world. Things like alarm clocks, traffic, dishes, laundry, the dentist . . . and the list goes on and on. But what if we look deeper than the petty things of this world that we have to endure? What about the hate we see in terrorism? The hate we see in racial prejudice, senseless violence, bullying, and lies that destroy?

The Bible says in Proverbs 6:16–19, "There are six things the LORD hates, seven that are detestable to him: haughty eyes, a lying tongue, hands that shed innocent blood, a heart that devises wicked schemes, feet that are quick to rush into evil, a false witness who pours out lies and a person who stirs up conflict in the community."

Letting go of hate is opening our hearts to love and living in harmony with everyone God created. We as believers are all brothers and sisters in Christ.

Dear Jesus,
Thank you for this day. Help me to let go of hate. Help me to . . .

Letting Go of Worry

The definition of worry is to give way to anxiety or unease; to allow one's mind to dwell on difficulty or troubles. To give way is to yield to something, to allow something or someone to be first.

So, my question for you today is: Are you allowing worry to control your thoughts and be first in your life? There is only one way to let go of worry, and that is to give it to God. He alone can calm any storm and give you the kind of peace you need to move forward, one step at a time.

"Do not be anxious about anything, but in every situation, by prayer and petition, with thanksgiving, present your requests to God. And the peace of God, which transcends all understanding, will guard your hearts and your minds in Christ Jesus.

Finally, brothers and sisters, whatever is true, whatever is noble, whatever is right, whatever is pure, whatever is lovely, whatever is admirable—if anything is excellent or praiseworthy— put it into practice. And the God of peace will be with you."
—PHILIPPIANS 4:6–9

Dear Jesus,
Thank you for this day. Help me to let go of worry. Help me to . . .

Letting Go of Our Own Agenda

We all have agendas. Our phones now remind us of our day-to-day agendas, filled with appointments and errands and things we like to do. We also have agendas that extend out over the year: trips we want to take, family to see, work events, and dreams we make when we have time to think about the future.

I've learned, though, that it is one thing to make an agenda and another to have it rule our life. We need to be able to hold on loosely enough to allow God to do a work in us and through us. We need to have the flexibility that if life changes course we can trust God and his plans.

> "In their hearts humans plan their course,
>   but the LORD establishes their steps."
> —PROVERBS 16:9

Dear Jesus,
Thank you for this day. Help me to let go of my agenda. Help me to . . .

Letting Go of Giving Up

If I listened to the little voice on my shoulder every time things get hard, I would never get out of bed in the morning. Sometimes it seems easier to just give up, but I'm here to tell you it's not. That is exactly what the enemy of your soul wants you to believe and where he wants you to stay camped. Not moving forward. Not experiencing all that God has planned for you.

In this world we often set a timeline that is unrealistic and unhealthy. While our perspective is narrow, God can see for miles in all directions. When things are hard and not going the way we want them to, we need to hold on and trust God and His timing. We need to believe that God can see just where we'll finally turn the corner and climb the long road we've been traveling to get to the top. And from this view, it will be amazing and worth it.

> "Let us not become weary in doing good, for at the proper time we will reap a harvest if we do not give up."
> —GALATIANS 6:9

Dear Jesus,
Thank you for this day. Help me to let go and not give up. Help me to . . .

Letting Go and Letting God

In December 2016 my mother suffered a stroke. I have had challenging things in my life, but my heart was so torn with her living in Arizona and me in Michigan. The feeling of helplessness was almost overwhelming at times, and all I could do was wait. I was able to go to be with her, but I now know the reason God gave me the words "Let Go" for 2017. I've had to let go and let God with so many things . . . with her care, her financial situation, medical bills, and just living day to day.

Looking back, God was so close—walking with us each step of the way. I can tell you today, with confidence, that when you let go and let God He will give you exactly what you need at the exact moment you need it. Do you believe that? Do you believe He loves you enough to provide your every need, even in the midst of the storm?

> "'Don't let your hearts be troubled. You believe in God; believe also in me.'"
> —JOHN 14:1

Dear Jesus,
Thank you for this day. Help me to let go. Help me to . . .

Letting Go of Gossip

It's easy to get caught up in talking about someone else. One thing leads to another, and before we know it we've gone from nodding along to adding our two cents. But this is not helpful to the person we're talking about or to the person we're talking to. How do we show Christ in our lives by going along with people?

It's hard to "speak up" by not saying anything at all, but I believe we're called to live not only by our words but by the things we do not say. Ephesians 4:29 says, "Let no corrupting talk come out of your mouths, but only such as is good for building up, as fits the occasion, that it may give grace to those who hear."

Letting go of gossip is holding onto love and being obedient to the way God calls us to live.

"'Do to others as you would have them do to you.'"
—LUKE 6:31

Dear Jesus,
Thank you for this day. Help me to let go of gossip. Help me to . . .

Letting Go of Letting Someone Else Define You

I was reading an article about Stedman Graham, partner to Oprah Winfrey. He spoke at a conference a couple of years back and said these words: "But I realized a long time ago: You can't let anybody else define you. Freedom is not about how other people define you, but how you define yourself."

I can't imagine walking in the shadow of someone like Oprah Winfrey, but I know I've let people in my life set limitations for me and saw myself through their eyes. When we do this, we're not seeing the bigger picture. If we could step back and see ourselves the way God sees us, we would never once doubt that we are special, we are blessed, and we are loved. I'm praying that today you will let go of what others may think about you and accept His love.

> "May God himself, the God of peace, sanctify you through and through. May your whole spirit, soul and body be kept blameless at the coming of our Lord Jesus Christ."
> —1 THESSALONIANS 5:23

Dear Jesus,
Thank you for this day. Help me to let go of someone else defining me.
Help me to . . .

Letting Go of Negative Thinking

I've had days when it was hard to find a positive thought—whether it's about myself and all the things that are wrong with me or about the world and how everything seems to be going wrong. Where do you think these negative thoughts come from when they come streaming in? I know it's the enemy. There is no place else he would like us to be than trapped under a heavy load of lies.

So, how do we stop him? How do we stop the cycle of negative thoughts? We need to pray and switch our focus to God above!

Paul wrote in Philippians 4:8–9, "Finally, brothers and sisters, whatever is right, whatever is pure, whatever is lovely, whatever is admirable—if anything is excellent or praiseworthy—think about such things. Whatever you have learned or received or heard from me, or seen in me—put it into practice. And the God of peace will be with you."

Today, rebuke the enemy and switch your focus from the horrible to the honorable. From injustice to justice. From lies to the lovely. Open up your clenched fist and welcome the peace that only God can give . . . and breathe.

Dear Jesus,

Thank you for this day. Help me to let go of negative thinking. Help me to . . .

Letting Go of Frustration When People Don't Share Your Beliefs

We've all experienced feeling frustrated when we can't convince someone to believe the way we do. Maybe it's a movie choice or a sports team preference—but what about religion or politics? Social media blew up during the 2016 presidential election, and I saw friends take opposite sides and say the cruelest things to each other, trying to convince the other to believe the way they did. Is this necessary? It feels like it is sometimes, trying to make our case, but it doesn't make it right.

When Jesus came, he didn't force people to believe in Him. He didn't get frustrated and call people names and march in the street breaking things and hurting people. He loved them, regardless of what they believed. His actions spoke volumes about who He was. To be like Christ, we need to do the same.

> "Dear children, let us not love with words or speech but with actions and in truth."
> —1 JOHN 3:18

Dear Jesus,

Thank you for this day. Help me to let go of frustration when people don't believe the same as me. Help me to . . .

MAY 30

Letting Go of Believing
You Can Never Change

We are almost to the end of this month. We've dug deep into the things that are sometimes uncomfortable to talk about and think about, especially when they are things we need to change. But don't believe for a second that you cannot do it. We can ask God for anything, and He especially answers our prayers when we are asking to be more like Him.

My prayer for you today is that you will be open to the things that God has spoken to you about and that you will not be discouraged. The enemy can be relentless with his lies, and he will want you to go back to old habits and ways. Pray each day for protection from the enemy and "be strong in the Lord and in his mighty power. Put on the full armor of God, so that you can take your stand against the devil's schemes" (Ephesians 6:10–11).

Dear Jesus,
Thank you for loving me. Please go before me and prepare a way. Protect me from the lies of the enemy and help me to be more like You. In Your name I pray these things. Amen.

Dear Jesus,
Thank you for this day. Help me to let go of believing I can never change. Help me to . . .

Letting Go

On May 1 we talked about the act of letting go . . . opening our clenched hands and lifting our palms to the sky and saying "God, I can't carry this anymore!"

I encourage you as you move through the rest of this year to continue practicing this exercise every time you are tempted to take something back. Continue to be open to what God wants you to let go of, and remember to live a surrendered life . . . the only thing we need to hold onto is God Himself!

Dear Jesus,

Thank you for this day. Help me to let go and let You work in my life.
Help me to . . .

June

OUR AUTHENTIC SELVES

"I praise you because I am fearfully and wonderfully
made; your works are wonderful, I know that full well.
My frame was not hidden from you when I was
made in the secret place, when I was
woven together in the depths of the earth.
Your eyes saw my unformed body; all the days
ordained for me were written in your book
before one of them came to be."

—PSALM 139:14–16

A Word

Going into each new year, I ask the Lord to give me a word. The word I receive is usually something I need to focus and work on, something that I still struggle with. This year the word that came to me was something I experienced while at church. Everything about my experience, including praying on my knees, the people who spoke, and the atmosphere around me made me think of one word: *authentic*. So, when I received this word for my own, I wanted to share it with all of you. What better way to come out of Lent and Easter and letting go than learning how to be more of ourselves and experiencing the fullness of how God created us to be.

So I invite you to look closely at your life these next 29 days. Be open to what God shows you, and be open to change. I look forward in anticipation to what He wants to do.

> "So God created mankind in his own image,
>   in the image of God he created them;
>   male and female he created them."
> —GENESIS 1:27

Dear Jesus,
Thank you for this day. Help me to be my most authentic self. Help me to . . .

The Definition

As we get started, let's look at what *authentic* means.

The dictionary's definition of *authentic* is: not false or copied; genuine; real and having an origin supported by unquestionable evidence; authenticated; verified.

The Bible has countless verses on being authentic, including Romans 12:2: "Do not conform to the pattern of this world, but be transformed by the renewing of your mind. Then you will be able to test and approve what God's will is—his good, pleasing and perfect will."

So, to be authentic we must be genuine, know where we come from (from God), and not be conformed to what the world thinks is perfect. We need to accept ourselves as we are and how God created us to be. Amen!

Dear Jesus,
Thank you for this day. Help me to not be conformed to this world.
Help me to . . .

Surrender

Imagine a young girl sitting on her bike ready to take on the world. She has a smile that is contagious and free and is concerned only about where she will go next. She had her mom gather her hair quickly into a pony tail before she raced out the door ready to take on an adventure. She didn't care what anyone thought, and she knew without a doubt that the Lord loved her unconditionally. I loved this girl. She was truly authentic!

So what happened to this girl? She grew up. She started caring about her appearance, what the scale said, and what people said about her, and she doubted that the Lord could really love her after everything she had done.

But one day, many years later, she cried out to Him, surrendering her life, turning over her brokenness, wanting to be authentic once again.

If this is you today, it's not too late. Only Jesus can affirm who you are, love you unconditionally, and help you to be all that He has designed you to be. He will forgive your past and restore your life. All you need to do is step out in faith and believe. If you're ready, read as your own the prayer below:

Dear God,
I know I'm a sinner, and I ask for Your forgiveness. I believe Jesus Christ is Your Son. I believe that He died for my sins and that You raised Him to life. I want to trust Him as my Savior and follow Him as Lord from this day forward. Guide my life and help me to do Your will. I pray this in the name of Jesus. Amen.

Dear Jesus,
Thank you for this day! Thank you for forgiving me. Thank you for loving me. Help me to follow You by . . .

The Mirror

What do you see when you look in the mirror? Maybe it's a failure as a husband or wife or a student in school. Maybe you see someone who has been let down time and time again by people you trusted. Maybe you see someone who is out of work and out of time or maybe . . . you no longer recognize the person looking back at you.

No matter the reason, you have run to this mirror for too long hoping to see a thinner you, a younger you, a happier you. But the answer isn't in the reflection—it's inside. The mirror has rejected me countless times, because it's how I see myself. We need to start seeing ourselves as God sees us, not as the world sees us. We need to start embracing who we really are . . . children of God; sons and daughters of the King!

> "But he said to me, 'My grace is sufficient for you, for my power is made perfect in weakness.' Therefore I will boast all the more gladly of my weaknesses, so that the power of Christ may rest on me. That is why, for Christ's sake, I delight in weaknesses, in insults, in hardships, in persecutions, in difficulties. For when I am weak, then I am strong."
> —2 CORINTHIANS 12:9-10

Dear Jesus,
Thank you for this day. Help me to see myself as You see me. Help me to . . .

God's Original

Here is a challenging question: Do you look for approval from others? Do you find your value in how well you do your job or from the perspective of your spouse or your children or your friends?

When we get affirmation from the people around us, we're no longer looking in the mirror but seeing ourselves through the eyes of someone else. This is fine when they look at us with love, but what happens when their opinion of us changes? What happens when they're in a bad mood or going through a challenging season and don't have a positive word for you? Did your value change? No. Did you change? Not necessarily.

To be truly authentic, we need to be original—our own original, the way God designed us to be. And when His opinion of us means more to us than anyone else's, we are traveling down a path of true freedom! We need to stay rooted in His love, because God's opinion of us will never change.

Today, use this Bible verse to remind yourself who you are: "I praise you because I am fearfully and wonderfully made" (Psalm 139:14).

Dear Jesus,

Thank you for this day. Help me to find my true value in You. Help me to . . .

The Lie

There was one lie I heard from the enemy that was the hardest for me to overcome. My name means beloved: adored, much loved, cherished, treasured, prized, highly regarded, admired, esteemed, and revered. But what I had heard for many years in my own mind was more like:

> Unworthy
> Undeserving
> Ineligible
> Unfit and unqualified.

To feel unworthy takes every good gift and damages it somehow before the heart even receives it. It creates a disbelieving spirit, so that the true intention never penetrates the surface. It bounces back and disappears altogether. It is the perfect lie to tell to accomplish the most damage. It's simple, direct, and layered with the exact ingredient used to destroy the recipient: disdain.

The enemy of your soul doesn't want you to be authentic. He doesn't want you to find your value in God. He wants you to struggle, day in and day out, never knowing your full potential and wasting your time searching for the things that will always leave you thirsting for more.

Jesus said, "'Whoever drinks the water I give them will never thirst. Indeed, the water I give them will become in them a spring of water welling up to eternal life'" (John 4:14).

My friend, hold true to the promise that you are a child of God. You are worthy. You are amazing. You have value. Today, be truly authentic!

Dear Jesus,

Thank you for this day. Help me to stop believing the lies of the enemy. Help me to . . .

Labels

Labels. They surround us everywhere we go. They are on our clothing, the way we describe the people around us, and how we describe ourselves. But what if there weren't any labels? The kind of clothing wouldn't matter, we would all just be people, and we could be ourselves.

Today, if you want to label yourself anything, let it be "authentic"! You were designed to be 100% original and fashioned by a one-of-a-kind Designer—God. Amen!

> "Your beauty should not come from outward adornment, such as elaborate hairstyles and the wearing of gold jewelry or fine clothes. Rather, it should be that of your inner self, the unfading beauty of a gentle and quiet spirit, which is of great worth in God's sight."
>
> 1 PETER 3:3–4

Dear Jesus,
Thank you for this day. Help me to not label myself or others. Help me to . . .

The Mask

For many years I hid behind a mask. I tried to be perfect and let everyone believe that I was "fine." But the truth was that I felt like I was damaged goods. I felt that I needed to pretend to be someone else, because no one would love me for who I really was.

But, of course, that was a lie. Jesus loved me for me and died on a cross to save me. I had to learn that to be authentic we need to be transparent. In those difficult times, instead of saying "I'm fine," we need to share with someone how we're really doing and ask for prayer. When we shine light into the dark areas of our life, we give God the ability to do His work in us and heal us from our brokenness. This was a hard lesson to learn, and I had to lose everything to learn it.

Today if you are hurting, reach out to someone and let them know, and ask them to pray for you! Don't live a lie anymore. We are all broken and hurting and need Jesus and each other.

"For everything God created is good, and nothing is to be rejected
if it is received with thanksgiving."
—1 TIMOTHY 4:4

Dear Jesus,
Thank you for this day. Help me to be transparent in my weakness.
Help me to . . .

Never Let Go

When I was in Guatemala, there was one little girl who left quite an impression on me, and I on her. She was smaller and frailer than the rest of the kids, and her face held little emotion. I saw her everywhere: on the road walking, by the house we were building, and at vacation Bible school with her mother. One afternoon when I was walking into the church to help, the ladies had already started and the singing was underway. I stood near the mother and the girl, watching as the little girl cried and tried to get free from her mom. The mom looked at me and nodded, and I wasn't sure what she was doing until she put the little girl down and let her run straight to me with her arms open wide. As I picked her up, she clung to me as tightly as her little arms could hold, and I was overwhelmed. I held her, feeling grateful, as we rocked to the music that was played.

There is only one word that describes this moment: *authentic*. I could see the distress on her face trying to break free from her mother, feel her little arms wrap around my neck, and know in my heart that this is the way Jesus loves us. This is something I will never forget, and I only hope that I will run to Jesus this way, holding on and never letting go.

Dear Jesus,
Thank you for this day. Help me to love like You and to live authentically and to never let go. Help me to . . .

Step by Step

One of the first hikes we took when traveling in Israel was in the desert. It was overwhelmingly beautiful, with a vastness that is hard to comprehend until you're walking in it. We started out at the top of the Makhtesh Ramon and climbed downward to the flat part of the Negev. We lined the mountainside, walking single file, zigzagging carefully over rocks at a speed that would accommodate the entire group. It was dry, so dry that our sweat evaporated, and it was only the shade from our hats that spared us from the scorching sun. We were like the Israelites, but with hats and sunglasses and water bottles. All forty-nine of us walked in, but seven were walked out—all three and a half miles in the 100 degree temperatures. Not forty years, but three hours. Some of us drank too much water early on and ran low before we made it out. Some experienced heat exhaustion, and their bodies just said that was enough. We complained and sweated and prayed, and all of us made it out, but not without experiencing a life alteration and a great respect for the Israelites, the desert, and how God answers prayers and gives strength when needed and when we ask.

I thanked Him for the breeze. I thanked Him for the strength to walk out not only with my own backpack but carrying someone else's and supporting my roommate on my arm. I felt the prayers from my family and friends back home as I put one foot in front of the other. I learned that day that we have to trust God step by step. God doesn't call us to a life of comfort and complacency; that is why He gave Israel to the Israelites. It's not an easy country to live in, and you need to depend on God.

To be authentic, we need to realize that we cannot do things in our own strength. We cannot doubt that God will provide for us, and we need to learn to trust Him.

Dear Jesus,

Thank you for this day. Help me learn to trust You completely. Help me to . . .

Listen

D o you hear Him? The still, small voice inside you guiding, protecting, encouraging, and telling you He loves you and to whom you belong? It's different from the other voices of this world—*loud*, discouraging, hateful, trying to convince you that you are not enough. Today, try to find a quiet space and listen. Listen for the one authentic voice: the Creator of the universe speaking to you and reminding you that you are His.

Whenever you feel unloved, unimportant, or insecure, remember to whom you belong!

> "Consequently, you are no longer foreigners and strangers, but fellow citizens with God's people and also members of his household, built on the foundation of the apostles and prophets, with Christ Jesus himself as the chief cornerstone. In him the whole building is joined together and rises to become a holy temple in the Lord. And in him you too are being built together to become a dwelling in which God lives by his Spirit."
> —EPHESIANS 2:19-22

Dear Jesus,
Thank you for this day. Help me to hear Your voice. Help me to . . .

The Word

How do we find ways to be our true, authentic selves? We find them by being in the Word every day. If you've never read the Bible and it seems overwhelming, start in the New Testament first. If you don't have a Bible, email me at info@ammiebouwman.com and I will send you one.

> "All Scripture is God-breathed and is useful for teaching, rebuking, correcting and training in righteousness, so that the servant of God may be thoroughly equipped for every good work."
> —2 TIMOTHY 3:16–17

> "The word became flesh and made his dwelling among us. We have seen his glory, the glory of the one and only Son, who came from the Father, full of grace and truth."
> —JOHN 1:14

Dear Jesus,
Thank you for this day. Give me a hunger to be in Your Word every day and to learn from You. Help me to . . .

You Are Mine

Once God showed me the changes I needed to make I was filled with guilt and remorse for the years I had made the same mistakes. But even while He was correcting me, He was whispering in my ear that He loved me, that He had redeemed me, and that I was His. He is the perfect Father. Allow Him today to speak into your life and to redeem you.

"Do not fear, for I have redeemed you;
    I have summoned you by name; you are mine."
—ISAIAH 43:1

Dear Jesus,
Thank you for this day. Help me to turn from my mistakes and live for
You. Help me to . . .

Members of God's Family

I was reminded one Sunday during a sermon that we are marked by God. We were created and designed for greatness and have been given a mission to amplify this hope and life to everyone. This is what I wanted to do. I wanted to declare to anyone and everyone who would listen that though this life is hard we are not alone.

God never promised that it would be easy being His authentic child. But we have His promise that we are citizens along with all of God's holy people. When it's challenging and difficult to walk this life separate from conformity to this world, we need to remember that we are members of God's family. We are accepted by the One whose opinion matters the most.

"Our citizenship is in heaven. And we eagerly await a Savior from there, the Lord Jesus Christ, who, by the power that enables him to bring everything under his control, will transform our lowly bodies so that they will be like his glorious body."
—PHILIPPIANS 3:20–21

Dear Jesus,

Thank you for this day. Thank you for walking with me. Help me to . . .

175

A Living Sacrifice

A prayer for today . . .

Father, thank you for knowing me
better than anyone else.
You know exactly what I need before
I even ask,
and your love heals my heart in ways
I cannot even
comprehend. Your gifts are
extravagant and your
beauty is all around me.
I love you, and I
offer my whole self
as a living
sacrifice for your glory.
Thank you
for today! Amen.

Dear Jesus,

Thank you for this day. Help me to hear from You today in a real and tangible way. Help me to . . .

The Great Commission

To be authentic is to understand what God has created us for. How are we uniquely designed to live this life for His glory and to further His kingdom?

We have all been commissioned, my friends. Our mission is to share the good news with our family, our neighbors, our coworkers, people at the grocery store, people we don't know. How do we do that? It's not just by our words but by loving them as Jesus loves us. It is carrying with us the fruits of the Spirit, which are love, joy, peace, kindness, goodness, faithfulness, gentleness, and self-control, and living out the message of Jesus Christ in our everyday life.

> "Then the eleven disciples went to Galilee, to the mountain where Jesus had told them to go. When they saw him, they worshiped him; but some doubted. Then Jesus came to them and said, 'All authority in heaven and on earth has been given to me. Therefore go and make disciples of all nations, baptizing them in the name of the Father and of the Son and of the Holy Spirit, and teaching them to obey everything I have commanded you. And surely I am with you always, to the very end of the age.'"
> —MATTHEW 28:16–20

Amen!

Dear Jesus,
Thank you for this day. Help me to be like You, and by my words and deeds to point people toward Your kingdom. Help me to . . .

It's Not Too Late

No matter how far wrong you've gone, you can always turn around. Do you believe this? Or do you believe that, if you've slipped into following the world and chasing after the earthly desires of your heart, it's too late? It is never too late! Don't believe the lies of the enemy. Today, rebuke him and hold fast to the fact that *you* are a child of God and you are loved!

> "If we confess our sins, he is faithful and just and will forgive us
> our sins and purify us from all unrighteousness."
> —1 JOHN 1:9

Dear Jesus,
Thank you for this day. Help me to let go of believing I can never change.
Help me to . . .

We Are the Clay

There are 34 verses in the Bible about sculpting and clay. My favorite is Isaiah 64:8: "Yet you, LORD, are our Father. We are the clay, you are the potter; we are all the work of your hand." But I was especially intrigued about this analogy when I came across an article on Bibleknowledge.com. It describes how actual pottery is made and how it fits into God's sanctification of us.

1. God needs the Word, symbolized by water, to be in us before He can start the sanctification process, just as the first thing a potter needs before working the clay is water.

2. You have to be properly "centered" in Christ. Once the clay is pliable, the potter will put it in the center of the wheel.

3. Sanctification is a slow, steady, and progressive process. The wheel turns slowly and steadily as the pot is molded.

4. Let God develop you to your fullest potential in this life. As the potter's hands work the clay, the lump starts to grow bigger and taller and takes shape in the potter's hands.

5. God knows exactly what He wants to do with your life, just as the potter knows exactly what he wants to make when He begins the process.

After I surrendered my life, to become truly what God had created me to be—my authentic self—I needed to be resculpted. Even though it was a challenging process, I love that God didn't just stick a band-aid on me. He fixed the broken parts, and now they are stronger than ever before.

I'm praying for *you* today! Praying that you will allow Jesus to show you the areas in your life where you need to be remade and let Him sanctify you.

Dear Jesus,

Thank you for this day. Please remake me into Your original design for me. Help me to . . .

Priorities

Sometimes I feel pulled in a million different directions. I have responsibilities to my family, to work, for taking care of our home, keeping up relationships with friends, taking care of my health, and making sure I get enough sleep every night. In the past these were my only priorities; I didn't make time for God, and my relationship with Him suffered. I didn't make time to do devotions every day. I didn't take time to be in the Word. I didn't carve out time to go to church on Sunday because there didn't seem to be enough days in the week. But that was one of the biggest lies I ever believed. I added up the amount of time I sat on the couch watching television. I added up the number of times I was on social media. I added up the blocks of time I was wasting trying to do things but unable to stay focused. In the end, there was a lot of wasted time, and I realized that if I wanted to have a relationship with God I would need to prioritize it. For me the proper prioritizing involved spending my first few moments a day with the Lord. It was making sure that I went to church on Sunday morning and scheduled other events afterward. Prioritizing was making a list and putting God first and family second and work third.

What does your priority list look like? Are you putting God first each day? Don't be like me and waste years fumbling through your day. If you do that, you won't be able to be your true, authentic self.

Dear Jesus,
Thank you for this day. Help me make You my number one priority.
Help me to . . .

Leave the Past in the Past

Sometimes it's tempting to travel down dark roads back to where we were broken and lost. The landscape is familiar and seems safe because we've been there before. But the Lord says in Isaiah 43:19, "See, I am doing a new thing! Now it springs up; do you not perceive it? I am making a way in the wilderness and streams in the wasteland."

My friends, leave the past in the past and live this new day! Let us all be grateful for a second chance at being our most authentic selves.

Starting tomorrow, we will go through each letter of the word *AUTHENTIC*. I will be breaking it down, letter by letter, creating a way to leave you with a daily reminder and giving you more space to write out how you would like to grow into your most authentic self. Remember, *you* are amazing—a son or daughter of the King!

Dear Jesus,
Thank you for this day. Help me leave the past in the past. Help me to . . .

A Is For . . .

Always listen to the Holy Spirit . . . who tells you who you are.

> "'I will ask the Father, and he will give you another advocate to help you and be with you forever—the Spirit of truth.'"
> —JOHN 14:16

I've tried listening to other voices in my life; to friends, family, coworkers, even the voices on the radio and on television. I've tried figuring things out on my own and spent a lot of time listening, but turns out all that time the whispers I heard were from the enemy of my soul.

Do you know who the Holy Spirit is? In a question on EveryStudent.com, titled "Who is the Holy Spirt?" the answer was this: "The Holy Spirit is not a vague, ethereal shadow, nor an impersonal force. He is a person equal in every way with God the Father and God the Son. He is considered to be the third member of the Godhead. When a person becomes born again by believing and receiving Jesus Christ, God resides in that person through the Holy Spirit.

A primary role of the Holy Spirit is that He bears "witness" of Jesus Christ. He tells people's hearts about the truth of Jesus Christ. The Holy Spirit was given to live inside those who believe in Jesus, in order to produce God's character in the life of a believer. In a way that we cannot do on our own, the Holy Spirit will build into our lives love, joy, peace, patience, kindness, goodness, faithfulness, gentleness and self-control.

So now that you know that you have this gift inside of you, will you listen? He is our truth and the only voice we need to hear.

Dear Jesus,

Thank you for this day. Please fill me with Your Holy Spirit, from the top of my head to the soles of my feet. Let me hear Your truth and remind me who I am. Help me to . . .

U Is For . . .

U nderstand where your truth comes from—the Word, not the world.

"All your words are true;
   all your righteous laws are eternal."
—PSALM 119:160

In an article written by Kenneth Copeland called "Why Is It So Important to Meditate on God's WORD?" he writes:

"So many born-again believers miss out on the world-overcoming victory that's theirs in Christ Jesus. They keep finding themselves 'under' the circumstances instead of 'on top,' and they can't figure out why. They've never understood a foundational truth about living the successful Christian life. They've never understood why it is so important to meditate on, or ponder and contemplate, the WORD of God."

Proverbs 4:20–22 says, "My son, pay attention to what I say; turn your ear to my words. Do not let them out of your sight, keep them within your heart; for they are life to those who find them and health to one's whole body."

Notice that according to those verses, when you "attend" to God's words they become "sayings." The Scriptures start talking to you. The Holy Spirit speaks them to you on the inside so you can not only see but hear the thoughts of God. If you'll make the decision to internalize those thoughts by saying them on purpose over and over again, eventually you'll catch yourself saying them without having to decide to do it. When that happens, your thinking in that area will have been converted. God's thoughts will have become your own.

Dear Jesus,
Thank you for this day. Help me to find my truth in Your Word. Help me to . . .

T Is For . . .

T he Lord has a purpose and a plan for your life.

> "'For I know the plans I have for you,' declares the LORD, 'plans to prosper you and not to harm you, plans to give you hope and a future.'"
> —JEREMIAH 29:11

This is not just a great verse to hang on the wall in your home or use as your screensaver. This is a promise from God! The enemy has whispered to you for too long that God doesn't keep His promises, and you've started to believe him. You need to remember that the enemy has come to steal, kill, and destroy and will do whatever it takes to make you believe that this is just another verse. Today, claim this verse as God's promise to you. The Lord *does* have a purpose and plan for your life.

Dear Jesus,
Thank you for this day and for Your truth. Forgive me for believing the lies of the enemy. Help me to stand on Your truth. Help me to realize that You have a plan for my life. Help me to . . .

H Is For . . .

Hope in the Lord.

> "'Have I not commanded you? Be strong and courageous. Do not be afraid; do not be discouraged, for the LORD your God will be with you wherever you go.'"
> —JOSHUA 1:9

There was a time when I stood before the mirror in the bathroom, with pills in the palm of my hand, and had no hope. I had hoped in myself, but failed daily because I could not overcome my mental illness. I had hoped in my husband, but he wasn't happy and couldn't lift me from my own sorrow. I had hoped in my children, but as much as they loved me they couldn't help me emotionally. I had hoped in the doctors, but all they could do was prescribe the very pills I held in my hand. There was only one person I had not hoped in, and that was Jesus. I had asked Him time and time again to take this from me, but He hadn't done so yet. I believed He didn't care. The enemy had me exactly where he wanted me . . . isolated, despondent, believing his lies and wanting to end my life.

What did I do? I finally hoped in the Lord. Whispering Jesus' name was all I had strength for. But His name was all I needed. I made it through that night and the next, and the next. And where am I today? I am healed! I am a new creation in Jesus Christ! I am free! It doesn't happen in our timing, but when we hope in the Lord it does happen!

Whatever *you* are going through today, all you need is Jesus! Keep His name on your lips. Do not be afraid because He is walking with you. He will be with you wherever you go.

Dear Jesus,

Thank you for this day. Thank you that I can call on Your name and You will hear me. Help me to find my hope in You. Help me to . . .

E Is For . . .

Eternal life is yours!

> "'Very truly I tell you, whoever hears my word and believes him who sent me has eternal life and will not be judged but has crossed over from death to life.'"
> —JOHN 5:24

It's easy to get caught up in this world and believe that this is all there is. It's hard to comprehend that we can live for eternity with Jesus in heaven. But why is this so hard to understand? Because we don't have the mental capacity. In our humanness, we cannot see the spiritual realm or understand the mystery. What we can do, though, is have faith!

> "The Sovereign LORD will wipe away the tears
> from all faces;
> he will remove his people's disgrace
> from all the earth.
> The LORD has spoken.
>
> In that day they will say,
> 'Surely this is our God;
> we trusted in him, and he saved us.
> This is the LORD, we trusted in him;
> let us rejoice and be glad in his salvation.'"
> —ISAIAH 25:8–9

Dear Jesus,

Thank you for the promise of eternal life with You! Thank you that all I have to do is believe in You. Help me today with my doubts and fears. Help me to . . .

N Is For . . .

Never underestimate the power of God!

> "He determines the number of the stars
>   and calls them each by name.
> Great is our Lord and mighty in power;
>   his understanding has no limit."
> —PSALM 147:4–5

There have been plenty of times where I underestimated the power of God! And each time He has proven me wrong. He had the power to heal me, save me, and give me a new life. He had the power to give me the words for the first book, the second, and now this one. He had the power for me to start For His Glory Ministry, build a church in Zambia, and help the widows and orphans. He has the power to do all of this and more, in my life and in yours. Believe in Him today and never underestimate His great and glorious power! Amen.

Dear Jesus,

Thank you for this day. Help me to never underestimate how powerful You are. You are the great I AM! Help me to . . .

T Is For . . .

The whole world will know that you are His.

> "'By this everyone will know that you are my disciples, if you love one another.'"
> —JOHN 13:35

It's amazing to feel love from another person. It radiates from them and comes out in their smile, the kind words they use, their whole demeanor. Our spirit recognizes this love, and so do others. Notice that Jesus didn't say everyone will know you are His disciple just by your saying that you are; it's by your showing that you are. Loving people is not easy, and we can't do it in our own strength. To love people we need Jesus in our hearts while we listen to the truth and wisdom of the Holy Spirit. Only then will they know we are His . . .

Dear Jesus,

Thank you for this day! Help me to shine my light for all to see. Help me to . . .

I Is For . . .

I nvest time each day with God.

> "'What good is it for someone to gain the whole world, yet forfeit their soul?'"
> —MARK 8:36

At the end, when we stand before Jesus and account for all of the things in our life, Jesus won't ask us how much money we made, how big our house was, or about all of the trips we went on. He'll already know how much time we spent with Him each day, if His word is embedded in our hearts, and how we lived for Him. So when you stand there, will you be confident? Will you know without a doubt that you lived for the Lord and for His glory, and not yours? Where are you investing your time each day?

Dear Jesus,
Help me. Lord. to make You first in my life. Create in me a hunger for Your Word and to live for You. Help me to . . .

C Is For . . .

C hoice—He gives this to all of us. Will you follow Him?

> "Now may the God of peace, who through the blood of the eternal covenant brought back from the dead our Lord Jesus, that great Shepherd of the sheep, equip you with everything good for doing his will, and may he work in us what is pleasing to him, through Jesus Christ, to whom be glory for ever and ever. Amen."
> —HEBREWS 13:20-21

Will you follow Him? Will you accept Him as the Center of your life, the Lover of your soul, the Healer of your diseases, the Savior of your heart? If so, tell Him today . . .

Dear Jesus,

Thank you! Thank you for chasing me and pursuing me! Thank you for never giving up on me. I choose You, Lord! Help me to follow You wherever you lead. Help me to . . .

Authentic

It's not always easy to look closely at ourselves, especially when we realize there are things we need to change. But to move away from the way the world sees us and focus on how God sees us will only make us stronger and happier and give us a more fulfilled relationship with Him. I pray that you will remember how incredibly special you are by remembering each letter of the word *AUTHENTIC* and all the ways you can be truly authentic in your daily living.

Dear Jesus,

Thank you for this day. Thank you for all the ways You've shown me that I am Your true masterpiece. Help me to live each day as my true, authentic self, a faithful follower of You, my Lord Jesus Christ. Help me to . . .

July

PROVERBS:
A MANUAL FOR LIVING
A PROVERB A DAY

*"For gaining wisdom and instruction; for
understanding words of insight; for receiving
instruction in prudent behavior, doing
what is right and just and fair."*

−PROVERBS 1:2–3

A Month of Proverbs | Proverbs 1

Chuck Swindoll, world renowned writer and pastor, writes, "Proverbs accomplishes something no other biblical book does: it simply compiles numerous short instructions for living an effective life on earth." So this month as we look at Proverbs, let us pray that God will give us wisdom as we start this journey, searching for knowledge. I encourage you each day this month to try to read one chapter. They are short and will take you only a few minutes. Doing this will not only grow your wisdom from reading Proverbs but grow your desire to read God's Word each day.

While reading chapter 1, pay attention to Solomon's words. In 1 Kings 3, I love how God comes to Solomon in a dream, after Solomon has offered a thousand burnt offerings on the altar. God says to Solomon, "Ask for whatever you want me to give you." Solomon asks God for wisdom, and God gives him that *and* riches and fame because of the nature of his request. He is so wise that people come from all over the world to hear Solomon's wisdom and see how he runs his kingdom.

Solomon's words in Proverbs 1:7 are amazing: "The fear of the LORD is the beginning of knowledge, but fools despise wisdom and instruction."

As you continue to read this first chapter, you'll see how important wisdom is and how we need it in our lives.

Dear Jesus,

Thank you for this day. Thank you for Your wisdom. Help me to receive it today. Help me to . . .

Moral Benefits of Wisdom | Proverbs 2

In *Talk Thru the Bible* Bruce Wilkinson and Kenneth Boa write, "Proverbs deals with the most fundamental skill of all: practical righteousness before God in every area of life. This requires knowledge, experience, and a willingness to put God first (3:5–7). Chapters 1–9 are designed both to prevent and to remedy ungodly life-styles."

While reading this chapter, look for ways that wisdom will benefit your life. I know from experience that without wisdom you will constantly be in search of your own "truth," and it will constantly change based on what you want to hear that day. Real truth does not waver. Real truth does not change. When we earnestly seek after God and His truth, we will want to follow Him and bend our life back to live in His light, His truth, and His wisdom.

> "If you look for it as for silver
> > and search for it as for hidden treasure,
> then you will understand the fear of the LORD
> > and find the knowledge of God.
> For the LORD gives wisdom;
> > from his mouth come knowledge and understanding."
> —PROVERBS 2:4–6

Dear Jesus,

Thank you for this day. Help me to seek after Your truth. Help me to . . .

Further Benefits of Wisdom | Proverbs 3

This is one of my favorite proverbs. When you're at the end of your rope, stressed by your day, searching for answers, filled with anxiety, angry or scared . . . , notice that the verse below begins with action and ends with a promise.

> "Trust in the LORD with all your heart
>> and lean not on your own understanding;
> in all your ways submit to him,
>> and he will make your paths straight."
> —PROVERBS 3:5–6

First — Trust in the Lord with all my heart.

Second — Admit, right now, that I'm not capable of making good decisions, and I don't understand what's going on. But I'm not going to react; I'm going to rest.

Third — With everything that I am, I will cry out to God. I will pray to Him and praise His name.

The Promise — He will direct my path.

While reading this chapter, look for all the arguments that persuade us to live righteous lives, and for the directions to do so, "for they will prolong your life many years and bring you prosperity."

Dear Jesus,
Thank you for this day. Help me to trust You with my whole heart.
Help me to . . .

Wisdom Is Supreme | Proverbs 4

"Above all else, guard you heart,
for everything you do flows from it."
—PROVERBS 4:23

There are three key subjects in Proverbs 4: the father speaks to his sons and tells them to get wisdom, avoid the wicked, and keep their hearts. I really like the way Rick Pina describes this chapter in *Unlocking the Power of Proverbs—Walking in the Wisdom of God*. He writes, "Solomon opens this fourth chapter with an invitation. It is as if he has proven to us by now (after 3 chapters) that he 1) walks in the wisdom of God, 2) has a sincere desire to share that wisdom with us, and 3) does so because he loves us, like a father loves his son/daughter. Solomon invites us to take a pause and to put ourselves in receiving-mode."

So, what can we receive today? While reading this chapter, see how Solomon instructs us as a father/teacher and warns us about the path of the wicked: "For they cannot rest until they do evil; they are robbed of sleep till they make someone stumble" (Proverbs 4:16). Today, receive Solomon's invitation. Get wisdom, avoid the wicked, and guard your heart.

Dear Jesus,
Thank you for this day. Thank you that You love me so much that You want what's best for me. Help me today to guard my heart. Help me to . . .

Warning Against Adultery | Proverbs 5

When reading this chapter, I was reminded of the many ways adultery can hurt our families, our future, and our relationship with God. Marriage is a covenant between a man and a woman, before God, and when we break that covenant there are consequences that we sometimes don't even think about until it's too late.

I was also reminded of the passage in John 8:1–11: "Jesus went to the Mount of Olives. At dawn he appeared again in the temple courts, where all the people gathered around him, and he sat down to teach them. The teachers of the law and the Pharisees brought in a woman caught in adultery. They made her stand before the group and said to Jesus, 'Teacher, this woman was caught in the act of adultery. In the Law Moses commanded us to stone such women. Now what do you say?' Thy were using this question as a trap, in order to have a basis for accusing him. But Jesus bent down and started to write on the ground with his finger. When they kept on questioning him, he straightened up and said to them, 'Let any one of you who is without sin be the first to throw a stone at her.' Again he stooped down and wrote on the ground. At this, those who heard began to go away one at a time, the older ones first, until only Jesus was left, with the woman still standing there. Jesus straightened up and asked her, 'Woman, where are they? Has no one condemned you?' 'No one, sir,' she said. 'Then neither do I condemn you,' Jesus declared. 'Go now and leave your life of sin.'"

Dear Jesus,

Thank you for this day. Thank you for wisdom. Thank you for the boundaries You put in place for our protection, and for the forgiveness You offer when we fail. Help me to . . .

Warning Against Folly | Proverbs 6

When reading this chapter, you will notice several principles the writer is trying to impress upon us:

- Don't be responsible for someone else's debt.
- Warnings against laziness.
- God will not always overlook our wickedness. There will be a day of reckoning, and it will come like a thief in the night.
- The Lord hates seven things.

"There are six things the LORD hates,
   seven that are detestable to him:
      haughty eyes,
      a lying tongue,
      hands that shed innocent blood,
      a heart that devises wicked schemes,
      feet that are quick to rush into evil,
      a false witness who pours out lies
      and a person who stirs up conflict in the community."
—PROVERBS 6:16-19

Dear Jesus,
Thank you for this day. Thank you for wisdom. Help me to be mindful
of Your ways and of the path You set out before me. Help me to . . .

Warning Against the Adulteress | Proverbs 7

I've never liked the word *adulteress*. It feels like a label that could stick with you, like the scarlet letter worn by Hester Prynne in Nathaniel Hawthorne's American classic by that title. But regardless of the word, there are several things in life that can attack a marriage or a relationship and make you lose focus on the other person, causing the relationship to spoil or be contaminated—hence the word *adulterate*.

There was a time in my first marriage when my husband and I adulterated our relationship with pornography. What started as a seemingly innocent ploy to "spice" up our marriage turned into a slippery slope, and we both fell off the mountain . . . each to our own demise.

In this chapter Solomon is not only talking about the act of adultery but about anything that can seduce you away from your spouse. When you cross that line, the consequences are endless, and the damage can be irreversible.

> "Now then, my sons, listen to me;
>> pay attention to what I say.
> Do not let your heart turn to her ways
>> or stray into her paths.
> Many are the victims she has brought down;
>> her slain are a mighty throng.
> Her house is a highway to the grave,
>> leading down to the chambers of death."
> —PROVERBS 7:24–27

Dear Jesus,

Thank you for this day. Thank you for wisdom. Help me to protect my marriage/relationship. Help me to . . .

Wisdom's Call | Proverbs 8

W hile reading this chapter you'll notice that, in the words of Charles F. Stanley, "wisdom is the capacity to see things from God's perspective and respond according to scriptural principles."

Why is wisdom so important? Andre van Belkum writes, "The Bible emphasizes that one of the greatest qualities we can possess is wisdom. The books of Proverbs and Ecclesiastes are replete with timeless advice, especially about the importance of wisdom: 'The beginning of wisdom is this—get wisdom. Though it cost all you have, get understanding.' (Proverbs 4:7, NIV). King Solomon, with all his magnificent wealth and possessions, understood the value of wisdom: 'For wisdom is better than rubies, and all the things one may desire cannot be compared with her.' (Proverbs 8:11)."

Dear Jesus,

Help me to desire wisdom, to want it more than anything else. Help me to have my eyes open to the things of this world that may detour me from You. Amen.

Dear Jesus,

Thank you for this day. Thank you for wisdom. Help me to . . .

Invitations of Wisdom and Folly | Proverbs 9

W hile reading this chapter, you will hear the invitations from both Wisdom and Folly. Observe the differences while they call you from the highest point in the city. One will bring you life, the other death.

"The fear of the LORD is the beginning of wisdom,
and knowledge of the Holy One is understanding.
For through wisdom your days will be many,
and years will be added to your life.
If you are wise, your wisdom will reward you;
if you are a mocker, you alone will suffer."
—PROVERBS 9:10-12

Dear Jesus,
Thank you for this day. Thank you for wisdom. Help me to . . .

Proverbs of Solomon | Proverbs 10

A proverb is a short, pithy saying in general use, stating a general truth or piece of advice. In *Talk Thru the Bible* Bruce Wilkinson and Kenneth Boa write, "Proverbs is the most intensely practical book in the Old Testament because it teaches skillful living in the multiple aspects of everyday life. Its specific precepts include instruction on wisdom and folly, the righteous and the wicked, the tongue, pride and humility, justice and vengeance, the family, laziness and work, poverty and wealth, friends and neighbors, love and lust, anger and strife, masters and servants, life and death. Proverbs touches upon every facet of human relationships, and its principles transcend the bounds of time and culture."

As you read chapter 10, notice these key verses on the source of wisdom. "Hatred stirs up conflict, but love covers over all wrongs, Wisdom is found on the lips of the discerning" (Proverbs 10:12–13).

Dear Jesus,

Thank you for this day. Thank you for wisdom. Help me to . . .

More Important Life Truths | Proverbs 11

When reading this chapter, notice its many important truths, including:

- God wants us to be honest in all of our dealings.
- It is very important not to be self-centered and caught up in pride.
- In this life we all have tribulations. But when we stand with God we will be delivered out of trouble.
- To make good decisions, we need wise council.

Amen!

"When pride comes, then comes disgrace,
   but with humility comes wisdom."
—PROVERBS 11:2

Dear Jesus,
Thank you for this day. Thank you for wisdom. Help me to . . .

Minding Our Words | Proverbs 12

I magine an inky hand, made up of negative words, gripped around the neck of a young boy. He's crying, looking at you with eyes of fear and extreme sadness. It would be hard to look at this image, but it's a true picture of what our words can do to someone . . . at any age.

There are many important truths you will read in this chapter, but there are one hundred verses in the Bible that talk about reckless words, including Proverbs 12:18: "The words of the reckless pierce like swords, but the tongue of the wise brings healing."

My question for you today is How are your words? Do they cut people down and put them in their place? Do they cause fear, shame, and sadness? Or do they affirm, nurture, and speak truth with love? If it's the former, there is still time to change. Ask Jesus to help you change the words you choose and how you say them. Ask Him to help you be quick to listen, slow to speak, and slow to become angry. Never stop trying, for Jesus says in Matthew 12:36–37, "But I tell you that everyone will have to give account on the day of judgment for every empty word they have spoken. For by your words you will be acquitted, and by your words you will be condemned."

Dear Jesus,

Thank you for this day. Thank you for wisdom. Help me to speak truth with love and choose words that affirm and nurture. Help me to . . .

Reinforcing Principles | Proverbs 13

hile reading this chapter, you'll see several key truths, among them:

- The contrast between the people who live wholesome lives and those who live worldly lives.
- The tongue can be a deadly weapon.
- Pride causes us to turn away from advice, while it's wise to accept it.
- The Word of God teaches us the way to eternal life.

"Those who guard their lips preserve their lives,
    but those who speak rashly will come to ruin."
—PROVERBS 13:3

Dear Jesus,
Thank you for this day. Thank you for wisdom. Help me to:

The Wise Woman | Proverbs 14

Today's reading starts out by describing the contrast between a wise woman and a foolish woman. Whether she is a homemaker who works at managing the home, caring for the children, and setting the tone of peace and love or works outside of the home helping to financially support her family, the responsibility is immense. She can be a wise woman and do all of this to the best of her ability, relying on God for strength, or she can be a foolish woman and not take into account the depth of her responsibility over the lives she has been entrusted with.

There was a time when I felt like the foolish woman. I was so wrapped up in my life, my illness, and what was happening to me that I neglected my family. I still did what I was "supposed" to do—made meals, cleaned the house, and took care of my children—but I didn't enrich their lives. I didn't realize the tremendous gift I had been given. While time passed and I eventually recovered, there are moments of deep regret that creep into my heart. I wish I would've done more.

Wherever you are on the path of your journey, please be mindful of the small window of opportunity we have. We can be wise and wholeheartedly embrace the responsibilities we have of caring for other people, or we can be foolish and not do so. When the window closes, you are left with the choices you have made. I pray they will be wise ones.

Dear Jesus,
Thank you for this day. Thank you for wisdom. Help me to . . .

Our All-Seeing God | Proverbs 15

"The eyes of the LORD are everywhere,
keeping watch on the wicked and the good."
—PROVERBS 15:3

I think this verse is one of the hardest things for us to comprehend. God sees us not only in full light, but under cover of darkness. He witnesses not only our grand moments, when we are helping someone in need, but our weak moments when we're cutting someone down. Not only when we're sitting in church singing songs to the Lord, but also when we're sitting in our homes, watching our televisions. I pray that today and always we may be mindful of our actions and remember that God is walking with us. Will we make some of the same choices if we do?

Dear Jesus,
Thank you for this day. Thank you for wisdom. Help me to remember
that You are always watching. Help me to . . .

More Truths to Live By | Proverbs 16

You will read many familiar truths in this chapter today, including

"Commit to the LORD whatever you do,
   and he will establish your plans."
—PROVERBS 16:3

"In their hearts humans plan their course,
   but the LORD establishes their steps."
—PROVERBS 16:9

"Pride goes before destruction,
   a haughty spirit before a fall."
—PROVERBS 16:18

Dear Jesus,
Thank you for this day. Thank you for wisdom. Thank you, Lord, for these words. Help me to write them on the tablet of my heart. Help me to . . .

The Essence of Relating | Proverbs 17

"A friend loves at all times,
and a brother is born for a time of adversity."
—PROVERBS 17:17

Adam Clarke's commentary in Studylight.org explains the verse above: "A friend loveth at all times—Equally in adversity as in prosperity. And a brother, according to the ties and interests of consanguinity, is born to support and comfort a brother in distress."

While I love this explanation, I love Jesus' directive even more: "'My command is this: Love each other as I have loved you. Greater love has no one that this: to lay down one's life for one's friends. You are my friends if you do what I command. I no longer call you servants, because a servant does not know his master's business. Instead, I have called you friends, for everything that I learned from my Father I have made known to you'" (John 15:12–15).

Are you this kind of friend? Would you lay down your life? Jesus is the greatest example, for He did that for us . . .

Dear Jesus,
Thank you for this day. Thank you for wisdom. Help me to love others the way You love me. Help me to . . .

The Safe Place | Proverbs 18

Do you have something or someone you run to when you're having a bad day? Maybe it's a friend you can call or text. Maybe it's a food that has your name written on it when you're at the end of your rope. Or maybe you go the cupboard, get out a glass, and pour yourself a tall drink. At the end of the day you have a text, an empty wrapper, and an empty glass. Do you feel better? Do you have what it takes to do two bad days in a row? Or three? What about a season of sorrow?

I love Proverbs 18:10, because it tells us where to turn: "The name of the LORD is a fortified tower; the righteous run to it and are safe." Many times in my life I have run to the arms of my Father. He is safer than a friend, more fulfilling than food or drink, and has the strength for me to run to Him hour after hour, day after day, year after year. His love never ends, and I always know where to find Him. He is my strong tower.

I encourage you today to hold onto this verse, let it sink into the depths of your heart, and remember where you can turn in your dark hours. Oh, how He loves you and me . . .

Dear Jesus,
Thank you for this day. Help me to see that You're my strong tower.
Help me to run to You. Help me to . . .

More Life-Altering Insights | Proverbs 19

There are many wise insights in chapter 19, among them:

"A false witness will not go unpunished,
   and whoever pours out lies will not go free."
—PROVERBS 19:5

"He who is kind to the poor lends to the LORD,
   and he will reward them for what they have done."
—PROVERBS 19:17

"Listen to advice and accept discipline,
   and at the end you will be counted among the wise."
—PROVERBS 19:20

"Many are the plans in a person's heart,
   but it is the LORD's purpose that prevails."
—PROVERBS 19:21

"The fear of the LORD leads to life;
   then one rests content, untouched by trouble."
—PROVERBS 19:23

Dear Jesus,
Thank you for this day. Thank you for these words. Help me to . . .

Trusting God | Proverbs 20

"A person's steps are directed by the LORD.
How then can anyone understand their own way?"
—PROVERBS 20:24

We may not understand everything while on this journey toward wisdom, but "trust in the Lord" is a consistent message. The word *trust* is found in 127 verses, 57 chapters, and 30 books of the Bible. If we can come away with anything this month, it should be to trust in the Lord. He will make our paths straight. Amen!

"Trust in the LORD with all your heart
    and lean not on your own understanding;
in all your ways submit to him,
    and he will make your paths straight."
—PROVERBS 3:5–6

Dear Jesus,
Thank you for this day. Thank you for these words. Help me to . . .

Heart Motivation | Proverbs 21

W hile there are many great truths in this chapter, I love verse 2: "A person may think their own ways are right, but the LORD weighs the heart." This is speaking of the false securities we all have. But while we can be self-deceived, doing what is right in our own minds and pleasing the flesh, God knows our heart. God determines our true motives.

There have been many times in my life when I have justified my own actions and walked my own way. I not only wasn't in His Word, but I didn't care to follow His wisdom. But now I know the truth. And when we know the truth—when we are in God's Word and know the path we are supposed to walk—how can we be self-justified? How then can we continue to make the same foolish choices for our life and chase after the desires of the flesh? We can't!

Galatians 5:19–21 says, "The acts of the flesh are obvious: sexual immorality, impurity and debauchery; idolatry and witchcraft; hatred, discord, jealousy, fits of rage, selfish ambition, dissensions, factions and envy; drunkenness, orgies, and the like. I warn you, as I did before, that thos who live like this will not inherit the kingdom of God."

My brothers and sisters . . . now you know! You know the truth. I pray that when God weighs your motives and searches your heart, He will find love, joy, peace, patience, kindness, goodness, faithfulness, gentleness, and self-control (see Galatians 5:22–23).

Dear Jesus,

Thank you for this day. Help me to know Your truth and live a life pleasing to You. Help me to . . .

Doing Life Together | Proverbs 22

"Start children off on the way they should go,
and even when they are old they will not turn from it."
—PROVERBS 22:6

I truly feel fortunate and blessed that as I grew up I was raised in the church. First Church of the Nazarene is where we went every Wednesday night, Sunday morning, and Sunday evening. I went to Sunday school and camp and even sang solos up front. We sang the old gospel songs like "What a Friend We Have in Jesus" and "Trust and Obey." I learned what it felt like to walk the long walk to the altar and kneel before the Lord to confess my sins. I learned about community and potluck dinners and sharing with others when times were rough. Every time I walked through those doors, I felt an overwhelming sense of belonging—what heaven might feel like someday living with fellow believers.

It was this foundation that carried me when I was growing up and brought me back when I had drifted away. Today, I praise God for His faithfulness and thank my parents for their dedication. I know that this verse rings true, and if today you are not part of a community of believers, I would strongly urge you to join one. This is not only the way to "train up a child" but a wonderful way to do life together.

Dear Jesus,
Thank you for this day. Help me to build up the foundation of belief in
others. Help me to . . .

Staying the Course | Proverbs 23

Halfway through chapter 22 and into chapter 23, you will notice that the writer changes direction in his writing. Instead of describing how we should live, he writes, "Do not . . ."

This is not just about reading a list of rules but about reading what the consequences for disobedience could be. Wisdom is defined as the quality of having experience, knowledge, and good judgment. If we have these, we will keep our heart on the right path.

> "Listen, my son, and be wise,
>   and set your heart on the right path."
> —PROVERBS 23:19

Dear Jesus,
Thank you for this day. Thank you for Your wisdom. Help me to . . .

The Foundation | Proverbs 24

"By wisdom a house is built,
and through understanding it is established;
through knowledge its rooms are filled
with rare and beautiful treasures."
—PROVERBS 24:3-4

I've seen both sides of this verse. When my parents were happily married and we were all going to church, the rooms of the house were overflowing with treasures. They built their foundation on the Lord and trusted in Him alone. But as the years went by and they drifted from His truth, a heavy air filled our home, weighted with tension and misunderstanding. It was nothing you could see, but only feel, as you walked from room to room. The treasures all but disappeared, and we were left with emptiness.

Going deeper than a physical house, what foundation are you standing on? Are you building yourself up with wisdom? Are you filled with all the things God tells us are treasures: love, compassion, hope, truth? Hold onto these verses today and think about ways you can strengthen your foundation and fill your rooms with the rare and beautiful gifts from God.

Dear Jesus,
Thank you for this day. Help me to stand firm on Your foundation of
wisdom. Help me to . . .

Metaphorically Speaking | Proverbs 25

W hile reading this chapter, you'll see that the style changes again as the writer makes comparisons, giving us a visual image:

"Like a club or a sword or a sharp arrow
>   is one who gives false testimony against a neighbor."
—PROVERBS 25:18

"Like a broken tooth or a lame foot
>   is reliance on the unfaithful in a time of trouble."
—PROVERBS 25:19

"Like cold water to a weary soul
>   is good news from a distant land."
—PROVERBS 25:25

And this one: "Like a city whose walls are broken through is a person who lacks self-control" (Proverbs 25:28). A man's spirit is who he is. If he loses control of his spirit, he has lost control of himself and is exposed and vulnerable to the evils of this world.

Dear Jesus,
Thank you for this day. Help me to understand Your truth. Help me to . . .

Stoking the Flames? | Proverbs 26

"Without wood a fire goes out;
without a gossip a quarrel dies down."
—PROVERBS 26:20

The imagery in this chapter is easy to see. This verse, reminding us that a fire cannot burn without fuel, describes how a quarrel will stop if its fire isn't stoked by words. Gossip can be the wood, adding fuel to any fire. Only we can put out the fire . . . or never start it in the first place.

Jack Hayford writes in *The Power of Words*, "Our words, often so recklessly spoken, carry more weight than most of us can imagine. In fact, hardly a week goes by in which you and I don't read or hear about some celebrity, elected official, or admired athlete whose words have gotten them into hot water. But the matter goes far deeper than being 'politically correct.' The power of words is fundamental to life—and can be instrumental in causing things to die."

How are your words? Are they building people up, or starting a forest fire causing irrevocable damage . . . ?

Dear Jesus,

Thank you for this day. Help me to understand Your truth. Help me to . . .

Our Earthly Future | Proverbs 27

While chapter 27 is filled with insightful verses and nuggets of wisdom, I particularly like verse 1: "Do not boast about tomorrow, for you do not know what a day may bring."

I resonate with this verse, because, just as I do, I see and hear many people planning their futures. We move in and out of our days based on the calendar on our phones, sometimes blinded by the fact that we truly don't know what the future will bring. We're surprised when something unexpected comes up and angered by the lack of control we really have. This verse is talking about how we don't know what the future holds . . . only God does. My favorite Scripture in the entire Bible that talks about this in James 4:13–15: "Now listen, you who say, 'Today or tomorrow we will go to this or that city, spend a year there, carry on business and make money.' Why, you do not even know what will happen tomorrow. What is your life? You are a mist that appears for a little while and then vanishes. Instead, you ought to say, 'If it's the Lord's will, we will live and do this or that.'"

Dear Jesus,
Thank you for this day. Help me to live in Your will and in Your timeline.
Help me to . . .

The Right Way | Proverbs 28

There are many truths in this chapter, including:

"Better the poor whose walk is blameless
    than the rich whose ways are perverse."
—PROVERBS 28:6

"Whoever leads the upright along an evil path
    will fall into their own trap,
    but the blameless will receive a good inheritance."
—PROVERBS 28:10

"Whoever conceals their sins does not prosper,
    but the one who confesses and renounces them finds mercy."
—PROVERBS 28:13

"Blessed is the one who always trembles before God, but whoever
    hardens their heart falls into trouble."
—PROVERBS 28:14

Dear Jesus,
Thank you for this day. Thank you for these words. Help me to . . .

Humility, . . . or Humiiation? | Proverbs 29

"Pride brings a person low,
but the lowly in spirit gain honor."
—PROVERBS 29:23

There are at least 36 verses on humility in the Bible. It is so important to remember that when we humble ourselves we lift others up. In Philippians 2:3–7 Paul writes, "Do nothing out of selfish ambition or vain conceit. Rather, in humility value others above yourselves, not looking to your own interests but each of you to the interests of the others. In your relationships with one another, have the same mindset as Christ Jesus: Who, being in very nature God, did not consider equality with God something to be used to his own advantage; rather, he made himself nothing by taking the very nature of a servant, being made in human likeness."

Dear Jesus,
Please humble me. Empty me of all the things that are of me and fill me
with You. Make me invisible, so that people can see You in my life. Help
me to lift others up for Your glory. Help me to . . .

Agur's Take on Wisdom | Proverbs 30

This chapter is a collection of proverbs written by an unknown scholar named Agur who was likely a student of wisdom at the time of Solomon. A note in the MacArthur Study Bible states, "Agur reflects humility in v1-4; a deep hatred for arrogance in v7-9, and a keen theological mind in v5-6. He goes on to talk about unwise behavior and points to the fact that sins can uniquely permeate a whole society or time period."

But I particularly like verses 8–9. This is how I would like to live—in balance, with the Lord always before me: "Keep falsehood and lies far from me; give me neither poverty nor riches, but give me only my daily bread. Otherwise, I may have too much and disown you and say, 'Who is the LORD?' Or I may become poor and steal, and so dishonor the name of my God."

Are you living in this balance?

Dear Jesus,
Help me to live in Your balance, with You always before me. Thank you
for these words. Help me to . . .

The Wise King and the Wife
of Noble Character | Proverbs 31

This last chapter contains the teachings of the godly mother of an unknown ancient king. One poem is called "The Wise King" and the other "The Wife of Noble Character." In "The Wise King" the author talks about speaking up for those who can't speak up for themselves and defending the rights of the poor and needy. In "The Wife of Noble Character" he describes all the things this wife and mother does to take care of her family and her great value: "A wife of noble character who can find? She is worth far more than rubies" (Proverbs 31:10).

I pray that you have enjoyed this month. I pray that you have enjoyed being in the Word each day and reading the many truths in Proverbs. As we continue on this journey, I pray that you will keep these truths in your arsenal and use them as a way to fight back against the enemy. He will continue to try to drown you with lies. But know that when you put on the armor of God you will "stand firm then, with the belt of truth buckled around your waist, with the breastplate of righteousness in place, and with your feet fitted with the readiness that comes from the gospel of peace. In addition to all this, take up the shield of faith, with which you can extinguish all the flaming arrows of the evil one" (Ephesians 6:14–16).

Dear Jesus,
Thank you for the the book of Proverbs. Help me to understand these many truths and use them as guidelines for my life. Help me to . . .

August

THE GREATEST OF
THESE IS LOVE

"And now these three remain:
faith, hope and love.
But the greatest of these is love."

–1 CORINTHIANS 13:13

The Greatest of These Is Love

In 1 Corinthians 13 Paul so eloquently writes of love. He not only describes what characterizes it—patient, kind, without envy and not proud—but points out that it never fails. And while three things remain—faith, hope and love—the greatest of these is love. Does that stand true in your life? Does love embody all of those things to you? Oftentimes it doesn't, and for the longest time I couldn't figure out why. That is, until God showed me that in our humanness we will always fail at love. No person will ever be able to love us the way we are designed to be loved. Only God can do that. And when we love in God's strength, not our own, that is when we can love others.

All this month we will look at the importance of love. We'll spend time reflecting on Scripture, read stories of others' struggles, and maybe finally understand what Jesus meant when He said, "'My command is this: Love each other as I have loved you'" (John 15:12).

Dear Jesus,

Help me to open my mind and my heart to what You want to say to me about love. Help me to love You, love myself, and love others. In Jesus' name I pray, Amen.

Dear Jesus,

Thank you for loving me. Help me to . . .

He First Loved Us

In the New International Version of the Bible, the word *love* is mentioned 319 times in the Old Testament and 232 times in the New Testament. Why is it so important? Because God is love. Biblestudytools.com writes it its commentary, "If we want the perfect example of love, it is in our creator God. Often, God's love is referred to as agape love which is the highest form of love that is selfless and sacrificial. It is steadfast, unchanging, and unconditional." And this theme of selfless love is reiterated over and over again throughout the Bible, especially in the verses below:

> "Dear friends, let us love one another, for love comes from God. Everyone who loves has been born of God and knows God. Whoever does not love does not know God, because God is love. This is how God showed his love among us: He sent his one and only Son into the world that we might live through him. This is love: not that we loved God, but that he loved us and sent his Son as an atoning sacrifice for our sins. Dear friends, since God so loved us, we also ought to love one another. No one has ever seen God; but if we love one another, God lives in us and his love is made complete in us."
> —1 JOHN 4:7-12

So the key is not that we love God, but knowing that He first loved us and sent His Son to die for us. When we truly understand that His love is a gift, we can share that gift with others.

Dear Jesus,

Thank you for loving me. Help me to understand how You love me and to share that gift with others. Help me to . . .

Loving Yourself

On a scale of 1–10, with 1 being the lowest and 10 the highest, how would you rate how you feel about yourself? Now answer honestly. For me, most days I'm above a 5. But there were years I circled the drain around a 1 or a 2 and felt that it would have been better if I'd never been born. Where did that self-loathing come from? At the time I thought it came from my mental illness, my failing marriage, and years of making wrong choices. But honestly, the enemy camped on my doorstep during those years, and I believed every negative thing he threw my way.

When I was healed in 2013, I was not only healed physically, but the scales fell from my eyes and I was able to recognize the torrent of lies the devil tells us every day. I would have to start battling for truth.

So, what is your number? What are you going through right now that makes you feel the way you do? The only reason my number is above a 5 today is that I know God loves me. I know that I am nothing without Him. I know that no matter what the world says about me, what my scale says about me, what the mirror says about me, what the enemy whispers to me, I am the daughter of the Most High King. And no matter what I think my number is, God sees me as a 10! Amen!

Dear Jesus,

Thank you for loving me. Help me to see myself the way You see me. Help me to battle against the enemy and recognize the truth. Help me to . . .

Loving Others

How do you show love to a difficult person? Oftentimes to connect with someone, especially when the relationship is challenging, you find out what they like and use that as a way to express the love you feel in your heart, even if it's as simple as making a sandwich. In *Rhythms of the Heart*, Phil Hook writes, "My mother and I did not 'mix.' I chose a typical teenage solution to the problem—silence.

I would leave for school in the morning, come home to eat, then leave again. When I was finally home late at night, I read books.

Invariably, my mother would come downstairs and ask me if I wanted a sandwich. I grunted my assent. She cooked egg and bacon sandwiches for me night after night until I left home for good.

Years later, when our relationship was mended, she told me why she had made all those sandwiches. 'If you would ever talk to me, it was while I made that sandwich,' she said."

Hook writes, "I've learned love is found in a constant display of interest, commitment, sacrifice, and attention."

Isn't that true? There are countless verses in Scripture where Jesus is the epitome of a consistent display of interest, commitment, sacrifice, and attention, even to those who don't love Him back. If we are to follow Jesus and the way He loves us, we must never give up on someone. Especially because Jesus never gives up on us.

Dear Jesus,

Thank you for loving me. Help me to love others the way You love me, and to never give up. Help me to . . .

What Is Love?

What is love? First Corinthians 13:4–7 describes it perfectly: "Love is patient, love is kind. It does not envy, it does not boast, it is not proud. It does not dishonor others, it is not self-seeking, it is not easily angered, it keeps no record of wrongs. Love does not delight in evil but rejoices with the truth. It always protects, always trusts, always hopes, always perseveres." Amen!

When I read this, I'm not seeing love as a feeling. I read each word or phrase as an action, something I need to do. And just like everything else in my life, I can't do these things—I can't love—without God.

We are going to spend the next 16 days breaking down this verse and inviting God into the way we love. Take this time to look at each of the relationships you have in your life—spouse, boyfriend/girlfriend, children, family, friends, and even strangers—and see how you can apply this verse. We are not looking at this as something to pass the time. We are looking at the greatest commandment we were ever given: ""Love the Lord your God with all your heart and with all your soul and with all your mind." This is the first and greatest commandment. And the second is like it: "Love your neighbor as yourself""" (Matthew 22:37–39).

Dear Jesus,

Thank you for loving me. Help me to love others the way You love me, and to never give up. Help me to . . .

Love Is Patient

Have you ever taken care of someone who is sick or in poor health? In many cases they are constantly needing something, they may not always have a receptive attitude, and they can complain about everything because they truly don't feel well. It can be a weary, thankless job and can leave you feeling hopeless, especially if the care is day after day.

I have seen firsthand the differences in my attitude when I ask God for strength and patience in these situations. When I love the way He loves me, He gives me everything I need in those difficult moments. Sometimes I need to pray every five minutes asking for patience, and the prayer that I send up is not only another petition to the Lord but an admission that I cannot do this in my strength. God is always faithful, and when I'm done I feel as though I've truly taken care of them with love.

If you find yourself in this situation, or any situation requiring patience with another person, pray to the Lord. He is the same Lord who loves unconditionally and has endless patience with us.

Dear Jesus,
Thank you for loving me. Help me to have patience with others. Help me to . . .

Love Is Kind

When I think about how love is kind, I'm reminded of the story in Luke 10 about the good Samaritan. It tells of a man who was making the desolate and dangerous trip from Jerusalem to Jericho and was robbed, beaten, and left for dead. A priest went by but did not stop to help him; so did a Levite. But when a Samaritan (a member of a group despised by the Jews) passed by, he took pity on the man and bandaged his wounds, put him on his own donkey, and traveled to an inn and took care of him.

What is interesting about this parable is that when reading it you would automatically ask yourself why the priest and Levite didn't stop to help. They were God-fearing men who wouldn't be expected to leave someone for dead. But the Samaritan was from another country. He didn't look at this man on the road and see a foreigner but someone who was in need. He showed kindness and took care of him.

How many times have we hesitated to show kindness to someone? When looking at them we weren't sure of their situation, how they got there, or why they needed help, or we hesitated to help because we were too busy, blamed them for their poor choices, or didn't want to get involved . . . so we didn't. But Jesus asks us to love one another and show kindness—not to judge. It is my prayer that today we can be quick to show kindness and love as Jesus loves us.

Dear Jesus,
Thank you for loving me. Help me to be kind to others, like the good Samaritan. Help me to . . .

Love Does Not Envy

I have felt envy in my life. I have walked a road where I peered into the windows of the lives of my friends and family and wanted what they had. I wanted a nicer home or a bigger boat or a stronger marriage. But the feeling I remember most walking this road was discontentment and an anger toward them for having what I did not. Envy not only started to destroy the love, but it clouded my vision and I began to make unhealthy financial choices.

Can you be content when those around you have more than you do? Can you love them and want what's best for them, even if that means that you go without? This is a choice we need to make each day. In God's strength we can love those who have more than we do. We can love them and be happy for them when they succeed, when they get new things, when they celebrate milestones. Each of us walks our own path, and when we can love without envy we can truly love with Jesus in our hearts.

Dear Jesus,
Thank you for loving me. Help me to love without envy. Help me to . . .

Love Does Not Boast

To truly love as Christ loves us, we need to worry more about what God thinks of us than about what others do. Sometimes this can seem challenging, especially when we're tempted to boast. Many times I have wanted to speak up and say "That was my idea," "I did that," "That was me," and I've had to remind myself that God knows. In Matthew 6:1–4, Jesus says: "'Be careful not to practice your righteousness in front of others to be seen by them. If you do, you will have no reward from your Father in heaven. So when you give to the needy, do not announce it with trumpets, as the hypocrites do in the synagogues and on the streets, to be honored by others. Truly I tell you, they have received their reward in full. But when you give to the needy, do not let your left hand know what your right hand is doing, so that your giving may be in secret. Then your Father, who sees what is done in secret, will reward you.'"

I'm praying that today we will boast only in the Lord. Amen.

Dear Jesus,

Thank you for loving me. Help me not to boast. Help me to . . .

Love Is Not Proud

I've never experienced anything more humbling than walking into a building to get food and having no money to pay for it. The atmosphere was different from a grocery store that streamed music in the background and had customers bustling about. People talked quietly here in the food pantry, gathering their boxes and picking out the food they needed. I struggled with how this would affect Jacob and Jessie and what they would think of me as their mother. And while a waterfall of emotions washed over me, pride could not have been one of them. I would've done anything for my children.

When you love someone, there is no room for pride. I will always remember that season in my life when I swallowed anything resembling self-regard and focused on what my children needed. God supplied all of our needs and gave me the strength to endure.

> "Do nothing out of selfish ambition or vain conceit. Rather, in humility value others above yourselves."
> —PHILIPPIANS 2:3

Dear Jesus,

Thank you for loving me. Help me to let go of my pride. Help me to focus more on the ones I love and on how You love me. Help me to . . .

Love Is Not Rude

How often are we tempted to lash out and say something rude to someone when we have been hurt or offended? Our ego, our pride, screams, "Don't take that from them! Don't let them treat you that way!" But as we watch Jesus move throughout the Gospels, we notice that He is never cornered, He knows when to ignore, He is not defensive, He's flexible, and He is never rude.

When you are tempted to respond to someone in a rude way, take a moment to breathe in and pray for wisdom. Words can never be taken back once spoken, and when we love others as Jesus loves us our desire will only be to lift them up, not to tear them down.

Dear Jesus,
Help me in my weak moments, when I want to respond out of anger or fear. Help me choose my words so I have nothing rude to say and only offer words of encouragement and truth. Remind me that I can do all things in Your strength, especially loving others. Amen.

Dear Jesus,
Thank you for loving me. Help me to not be rude but to love others as You love me. Help me to . . .

Love Is Not Self-Seeking

Never once in the Bible will you read "You'll do this if you love me." Yet so much of our foundation is built on this lie. How did we miss the fundamental truth that love is not self-seeking?

Part of this misconception comes from our feeling that we are not enough. And when we are not enough, we need to prove our love by doing what we're asked, even when the person who is asking does not have our best intentions in mind, but only theirs.

If we are to follow Jesus' example, we need to love and be loved, as He loved us—unconditionally, without ulterior motive, sacrificially, and prayerfully—relying on the Father.

If you are currently in a relationship where you're being told or you're the one saying "You'll do this if you love me," remember who loved you first and who knows your name. Let Jesus be your example that love is not self-seeking.

Dear Jesus,

Thank you for loving me, unconditionally and without ulterior motive. Help me to love others as You love me. Help me to . . .

Love Is Not Easily Angered

Did you know that anger is a secondary emotion? Oftentimes anger comes when we feel hurt, afraid, rejected, frustrated, or humiliated. We tend to use anger as a way of covering up those vulnerable feelings and striking out at the one who has brought them up.

In Jesus' life there were lots of reasons for anger. He was regularly in uncomfortable situations, surrounded by crowds of people who could have easily hurt him, frustrated with His disciples for not understanding who He really was, and rejected by the very followers who supposedly loved Him. But He wasn't angry. He was confident in His mission and in the One who had sent Him, His Father.

So many times I have reacted in anger, not giving myself a minute to think things through, assess the situation, or pray for strength. What about you? What can you now do differently, loving those around you as Jesus does?

Dear Jesus,
Thank you for loving me. Thank you for being the perfect example of how I should love others. Help me to not be easily angered. Help me to . . .

Love Keeps No Record of Wrongs

I have made plenty of mental lists in my life. One of them was definitely the list of indiscretions my husband had done against me. My list included the times he forgot important things, when he had harsh words, when he told someone something I had shared with him in confidence, fought with the kids . . . And one page turned into two and then three . . .

But at one Sunday morning service I was reminded that Jesus tells us to forgive each other, just as Christ forgave us, and that as far as the east is from the west, so far has He removed our transgressions from us. And most importantly, "If you forgive other people when they sin against you, your heavenly Father will also forgive you. But if you do not forgive others their sins, your Father will not forgive your sins" (Matthew 6:14–15).

My carefully constructed list of infractions would need to be destroyed. I didn't want God to keep track of all the things I had done wrong in my life. I wanted His complete forgiveness and love, and I wanted to love others in the same way He loved me. Are you ready to destroy *your* list? Are you ready to be set free?

Dear Jesus,
Thank you for loving me. Thank you for forgiving me for all my sins and for not keeping record of my wrongs. Help me to love others that same way. Help me to . . .

Love Does Not Delight in Evil

At first glance, you might think this is an easy one. I mean, who wants to delight in evil? Merriam-Webster's definition of evil is: morally reprehensible; sinful, wicked, causing harm. Wikipedia's definition of evil, according to a Christian worldview, is any action, thought, or attitude that is contrary to the character or will of God.

For me, this makes things a bit more complicated. I have found myself many times having an attitude that is contrary to the character of God, and I know I have delighted in it. I have loved feeling the self-righteous anger wash over me and believe I was right. I have loved talking about another person, convincing myself I had their best interest in mind. I have loved seeing someone else "get what they had coming to them," feeling that justice had been served. But is this how God loves me? Is this how God calls me to love others? I know that answer is no.

So how do we love as God loves us, not delighting in evil? We practice daily what is written in Philippians 4:8: "Finally, brothers and sisters, whatever is true, whatever is noble, whatever is right, whatever is pure, whatever is lovely, whatever is admirable—if anything is excellent or praiseworthy—think about such things."

Dear Jesus,

Thank you for loving me. Help me to have a heart after Yours, and to not delight in evil. Help me to . . .

Love Rejoices With Truth

Truthfulness is an important aspect when living a life like Christ's. It is not only one of the Ten Commandments, but Jesus talks about it when giving the Sermon on the Mount: "'All you need to say is simply "Yes" or "No"; anything beyond this comes from the evil one'" (Matthew 5:37).

But why do you think telling the truth is so important? Some people think there is nothing wrong with enhancing their account with some minor fabrications, while others have no problem prevaricating their entire story. For me, I've seen firsthand what a lie can do to a relationship, and this is why I believe love rejoices with truth.

When your yes is yes, and your no is no, not only is there peace and trust, but those who love and rely on you can let down their walls and be vulnerable and know they don't have to be on guard trying to discern the meaning behind your words. And when truthfulness is a foundation for living your life, it allows you to believe other truths and ideas and not be leery. God knew it would be a crucial component in how we live our lives and spelled it out for us in the beginning. Today, rejoice in truthfulness. It will set you free!

Dear Jesus,

Thank you for loving me. Let my yes be yes, and my no, no. Help me to . . .

Love Always Protects

In his book *The Ten Laws of Lasting Love*, Paul Pearsall describes a moment in his battle with cancer when his wife showed him how love always protects. He writes:

> "Any time a doctor came with news of my progress, my wife would join with me in a mutual embrace. The reports were seldom good during the early phases of my illness, and one day a doctor brought particularly frightening news. Gazing at his clipboard, he murmured, 'It doesn't look like you're going to make it.'
>
> Before I could ask a question of this doomsayer, my wife stood up, handed me my robe, adjusted the tubes attached to my body and said, 'Let's get out of here. This man is a risk to your health.' As she helped me struggle to the door, the doctor approached us. 'Stay back,' demanded my wife. 'Stay away from us.'
>
> As we walked together down the hall, the doctor attempted to catch up with us. 'Keep going,' said my wife pushing the intravenous stand. 'We're going to talk to someone who really knows what is going on.' Then she held up her hand to the doctor. 'Don't come any closer to us.'
>
> The two of us moved as one. We fled to the safety and hope of a doctor who did not confuse diagnosis with verdict. I could never have made that walk toward wellness alone."

Dear Jesus,
Thank you for loving me. Please guard me with Your angels and protect me from evil. Help me to . . .

Love Always Trusts

I remember my childhood like it was yesterday. That feeling of innocence and knowing certain things to be true. Like when you open the refrigerator door trusting there will be food; turn on the switch knowing there will be light; or watch a hand raise knowing it will come down with love. I loved, and therefore I trusted; I had no reason to believe otherwise.

Until the day came when we opened the refrigerator door and there was nothing. This was just the beginning of so many things changing in my world: my parents' marriage, where I would live, how I would look at life. But this death to innocence, while it happens to so many, is part of living in this world full of sin. God's original design was a world full of love and peace and trust. Just as we can't live this life in our own strength, we cannot love without God and we cannot trust without love. When we build our foundation on what we know to be true in this world, we will inevitably be let down. But when we build our foundation on God, this will allow us to cultivate a strong, healthy spiritual life in which love always trusts, no matter the circumstances.

Dear Jesus,

Thank you for loving me. Thank you for walking with me. So much has happened in my life, and it's hard for me to trust. But help me, Lord, to trust in You. Be my foundation. Help me to build my life on You. Help me to . . .

Love Always Hopes

Hope is defined as "a feeling of expectation and desire for a certain thing to happen." It could be an aspiration, desire, wish, expectation, ambition, aim, or goal. In my own life, I have hoped for many things and had hope in many people. But just like everything that we try to do in our own strength, hoping for something day after day, year after year and not seeing consistent results can cause you to grow weary.

It can grow a garden of bitterness and resentment, and before long you lose all hope.

But if you put your hope in Jesus Christ and trust that He can do *all* things in His timing and for His glory, you will never lose hope. You will be able to step back and continually pray and rest assured that if something is in His will, it will happen. Instead of bitterness and resentment, your garden will be blooming with faith, hope, and love. It is my prayer that you believe that today!

Dear Jesus,
Thank you for loving me. Let my hope rest in You, and help me trust that You can do all things in Your timing and for Your glory. Help me to . . .

Love Always Perseveres

My husband and I have had to work through many stressful things in our relationship. Besides being a second marriage for us both, which has brought its own unique set of complications, we have struggled with communication. When you have trouble communicating, it's challenging to talk out the hot topic issues, like dealing with teenagers or moving your mother in to live with you or starting a ministry.

But despite the challenges, even when it was tempting to give up and throw in the towel, there was this promise that we clung to: love always perseveres. Even when we can't do our marriage in our own strength, Jesus is walking with us. We are learning, instead of leaving prayer as a last resort, to pray for each other daily and to pray *with* each other. When you keep Jesus in the center of your marriage, your relationships, and your life, He can calm any storm, resolve any issue, heal any wound. Love always perseveres when Jesus is there, guiding you on.

What about you? Do you believe that love always perseveres? If not, have a conversation with Jesus today. Give Him your pain, your distrust, your wounds, and lay them at the foot of the cross.

Dear Jesus,
Thank you for loving me. Help me to trust in You and know that love always perseveres. Help me to . . .

Love Never Fails

What do you think about when you read this assertion? Maybe it's a hard clause to read out loud because love has failed you many times. Maybe it was a parent or a grandparent, a spouse, a best friend, your children—maybe you even believe God failed you. But the truth, though it's sometimes hard to see, is that God's love for us never fails and never ends. He was there in the beginning. He breathed life into us. He has cared for us and loved us. He sent His Son to die on the cross to save us from our sins and is one day coming back to take us home.

It is our human nature that fails us. It is the way we've learned to love each other, passing it on from generation to generation. It is all the lies we believe from the enemy and all the sin in this world that have made us believe that love invariably fails us, . . . and so does God.

I challenge you today to ask God to show you how much He loves you. And I challenge you to be patient and keep asking until He responds. Open your heart and your mind to hear His voice. He will not fail you, because His love never fails.

> "I am convinced that neither death nor life, neither angels nor demons, neither the present nor the future, nor any powers, neither height nor depth, nor anything else in all creation, will be able to separate us from the love of God that is in Christ Jesus our Lord."
> —ROMANS 8:38–39

Dear Jesus,
Thank you for loving me. Help me to trust in You and know that Your love never fails. Help me to . . .

To Feel His Love

I scroll through countless posts on Facebook and Instagram, and my heart is broken. There is a myriad of young people out there saying they wish they could die; countless posts of themselves in pictures looking for validation, looking for a heart-shaped "like" or a thumbs up. They question their appearance, their sexual orientation, their purpose. Is this their future? How do we help them feel God's love? How do we show God's love to a generation living their lives connected to a hand-held device?

We can feel God's love through the words and actions of other believers. We can feel His love through a glorious sunrise or the way He paints the evening sky at the end of the day. We can feel His love by thinking of the cross and how Jesus died so we can have life and have it to the fullest.

Today, help show God's love to someone, especially the younger generation trying to live in this world. Encourage them, mentor them, love them the way Jesus loves us. Help them to feel His love.

> "Whoever does not love does not know God, because God is love. This is how God showed his love among us: He sent his one and only Son into the world that we might live through him. This is love: not that we loved God, but that he loved us and sent his Son as an atoning sacrifice for our sins. Dear friends, since God so loved us, we also ought to love one another. No one has ever seen God; but if we love one another, God lives in us and his love is made complete in us."
>
> —1 JOHN 4:8–12

Dear Jesus,
Help me to love others the way You love me. Help me to show our future generation their future. Help me to . . .

Grateful for Love

I lost my grandfather in June of 2017. He wasn't the kind of man to say "I love you" very often, so when he did my heart grabbed those words right from the air and I held them close. He was always light-hearted and liked to tell jokes, and he would sometimes tease my brother and me in a gentle, fun way. He was reliable and friendly and loyal to his family, and I knew he loved me very much.

It was also obvious that he loved my grandmother; that would show in the simple things like grabbing her hand to walk into a restaurant, or how he would look at her when she was busy in the kitchen. I knew way back when I was little that I wanted to be loved like that.

He also loved the Lord, and it showed when he prayed at meals and family events. His voice would catch and would be thick with emotion, and you could hear every grateful praise, every loving thought that went straight to heaven's ears.

I feel grateful for the privilege of having known a man like this. I feel grateful to be called his granddaughter. If you know someone like this, let them know how you feel. Thank the Lord above for them. And know that the "greatest of these" is love . . .

Dear Jesus,
Thank you for loving me. Thank you for the gift of family and for those
people who love me. Help me to . . .

Love Restores

When I was eleven years old my parents got a divorce. This was devastating for me, and though I didn't show it on the outside it shaped my young heart in ways I wouldn't understand until I was much older and married myself. Love for me was not the "greatest of these," and I couldn't possibly see God's restoring love in my parents' lives . . . until one Easter Sunday. Fast forward 36 years to one spring afternoon when everyone was over for Easter dinner and to celebrate my daughter's birthday—and I mean everyone. Shortly after everyone arrived, I looked over and saw my mom hugging my step-mom and my dad hugging my mom and my mom hugging my grandma. It was an authentic, real love that had Jesus written all over it, and in that moment I knew. God does restore! It is not always in our timing, but when it comes it is so sweet. His love can do all things! Do you believe that today? If you don't, hold onto this image. And if you want to see your situation change, start praying fervently to the Lord, and trust that restoration will come in His timing and for His glory. Amen!

Dear Jesus,

Thank you for loving me. Today I give You my situation, and I pray for restoration. Help me to trust you, Lord, in Your timing. Help me to . . .

Love in Action

We spoke at the beginning of the month about love being an action. Here is yet another example of that truth. J. Allan Peterson, in *The Myth of the Greener Grass,* writes:

> "Newspaper columnist and minister George Crane tells of a wife who came into his office full of hatred toward her husband. 'I do not only want to get rid of him; I want to get even. Before I divorce him, I want to hurt him as much as he has me.'
>
> Dr. Crane suggested an ingenious plan. 'Go home and act as if you really loved your husband. Tell him how much he means to you. Praise him for every decent trait. Go out of your way to be as kind, considerate, and generous as possible. Spare no efforts to please him, to enjoy him. Make him believe you love him. After you've convinced him of your undying love and that you cannot live without him, then drop the bomb. Tell him that you're getting a divorce. That will really hurt him.'
>
> And she did it with enthusiasm. Acting 'as if.' For two months she showed love, kindness, listening, giving, reinforcing, sharing. When she didn't return, Crane called. 'Are you ready now to go through with the divorce?'
>
> 'Divorce!' she exclaimed. 'Never! I discovered I really do love him.' Her actions had changed her feelings. Motion resulted in emotion."

Is there someone you "feel" you no longer love? Try "loving" them with action. Do something kind, say a nice word, pray for them and for you to change your heart. Love in action and let God do the rest.

Dear Jesus,

Thank you for loving me. Help me to love. Help me to . . .

Love Is a Choice

Mother Teresa was born in 1910 and lived a life dedicated to helping the poor. She was considered one of the twentieth century's greatest humanitarians and won the Nobel Prize for Peace in 1979.

Mother Teresa's faith life was complicated. She says she sometimes didn't believe in God. "But she practiced," as Pascal-Emmanuel Gobry writes in his article on her in *The Week*, "what a friend of mine once called 'the faith of the body', as opposed to the 'faith of the mind', a concept captured by the proverb 'Act as though ye had faith, and faith shall be given to you.'"

I believe this is the same for love. There are times we will not feel love toward our spouses, family, friends, and especially strangers. We'll want to act in the flesh, and when we do this we are acting out of our tiredness, our bad day, our attitude, our own strength. To love someone is a choice we need to make day after day. Remember that when we do, God will give us His strength to love as He loves us. If you have doubts that you can do this, then look to the example of Mother Teresa. Before her death in 1997 she had helped hundreds of thousands of people in over 25 countries around the world.

Dear Jesus,

Thank you for loving me. Help me to love others even when I don't have the strength to do it on my own. Help my love to be an action. Help me to . . .

Looking Back at Love

When I think about love, I think about the way I have watched Jesus love me over the years. In the moment, in the thick of my despair, it was sometimes hard to see it. But when I look back over the hills and valleys I have climbed, I have seen where He's walked with me, where He's gone before me and prepared the way, and where He's carried me. His love is never changing, always encouraging, ever hopeful, never conditional, and always truthful. He's always listening, always guiding, always teaching me to be more like Him. He's Father, husband and friend, the beginning and the end, the great I AM.

Today, think back over your life. Have you seen Him? Have you felt His loving embrace in your life, heard His encouraging words? His voice resonates through a stranger's and His love through a hug from a friend. He has always been there, sometimes gently knocking for you to let Him in, at other times opening wide the doors and windows of your life to let the Son shine in.

Praise Him today. Tell Him how you feel. He loves you dearly, and if you don't believe it . . . look at His hands and His feet.

Dear Jesus,

Thank you for loving me. Today I praise You and give You all the glory. Thank you for walking with me and showing me every day that I am Yours. Help me to open my eyes so I can see more clearly. Help me to . . .

Grace in Love

How do you love someone who stumbles? How do you walk beside them and encourage them? In a *Leadership* profile of pastor and author Stu Weber, Dave Goetz writes,

> "Growing up, Weber developed a temper, which blossomed in high school and college. 'And then I went in the military,' Weber said, 'which doesn't do a lot to curb your temper and develop relational skills.'
>
> Early in his ministry, he stopped playing church-league basketball altogether; his temper kept flaring, embarrassing himself and the church. A decade passed. . . .
>
> Then his oldest son made the high school varsity basketball squad. 'I began living my life again through my son.' Weber terrorized the referees. . . . He received nasty letters from church members, who, he says now, 'were absolutely right on.'
>
> But then he got another note: 'Stu, I know your heart. I know that's not you. I know you want to live for Christ and his reputation. And I know that's not happened at these ballgames. If it would be helpful to you, I'd come to the games with you and sit beside you.'
>
> It was from one of his accountability partners.
>
> 'Steve saved my life,' Weber said. 'It was an invitation, a gracious extension of truth. He assumed the best and believed in me.'"

And isn't this how Jesus loves us? Shouldn't we extend the same grace to others? Think of what would happen if we did . . .

Dear Jesus,
Thank you for loving me. Help me to love those who stumble. Help me to . . .

The Beginning of Love

Do you ever wonder when "love" first happened? Was it in the garden with Adam and Eve? Was is it when God spared Adam and Eve when they disobeyed Him and ate from the Tree of Knowledge?

I believe love has always been here. I believe it has been here from the very beginning . . . In the beginning God created the heavens and the earth. He created day and night, separated water from sky, and created dry ground and seas. He made vegetation on the land and stars and planets in the sky. He filled the water with living creatures and the sky with birds, and blessed them. He created living creatures and wild animals and livestock, and then He created man and woman in His image, to rule over the fish of the sea and the birds of the air, over the livestock, over all the earth. When He finished His work by the seventh day, He rested. He blessed the day and made it holy.

We praise You today, Lord, Creator of the heavens and the earth! You are good, and Your love endures forever! Amen.

Dear Jesus,
Thank you for loving me from the very beginning. Help me to . . .

Sacrifice in Love

"'Greater love has no one that this:
to lay down one's life for one's friends.'"
—JOHN 15:13

The greatest example of love we have ever witnessed is what Jesus did for us on the cross. He took on all of our sin, all of our shame, all of our hurt, all of our pain, and nailed it to the cross. He died the death of a criminal, a sentence that was meant for you and me, and did so because He loves us.

If, today, you are still not believing that you are loved, or could love others the way Jesus loves, rebuke the enemy and his lies. You are precious and dearly loved, and Jesus is knocking on the door of your heart to tell you so.

Dear Jesus,

Thank you for loving me. I pray today that You will guard me with Your angels and protect me from evil and help me to rebuke the enemy and his lies. Help me to know without a doubt how much You love me. Help me to . . .

The Greatest Example of Love

All this month we have looked at the importance of love. We spent time reflecting on Scripture and reading stories of others who struggled and overcame, and now hopefully have a better understanding of what Jesus meant when he said, "'My command is this: Love each other as I have loved you'" (John 15:12).

We've learned that no person will ever be able to love us the way we are designed to be loved. Only God can do that. And when we love in God's strength, not our own, that is when we can love others.

I pray that today you will put the past in the past and move forward with your new truth: the greatest example we've ever had of how to love and be loved is in Jesus Christ. Amen!

Father God, Lord Jesus, Holy Spirit,
Thank you for this month. Help me to remember when things become challenging and hard that I can love in action, if not in feeling. Help me to love in Your strength, not mine. Help me to love those who stumble, those who are challenging to love, those who are family and those who are strangers. Help me to extend Your grace and love the way You love me. In Jesus' name I pray, Amen.

Dear Jesus,
Thank you for loving me. Help me, Lord, to . . .

September

HALLELUJAHS IN THE HARD TIMES

*"Then I heard what sounded like a great multitude,
like the roar of rushing waters and like loud peals of thunder,
shouting: 'Hallelujah! For the LORD God Almighty reigns.'"*

—REVELATION 19:6

Are You Listening?

Do you hear Him? The still small voice inside guiding, protecting, encouraging, telling you He loves you? It's different from the other voices of this world . . . *loud*, discouraging, hateful, trying to convince you that you are not enough.

Sometimes it takes everything we have to just get out of bed and do another day. But there is a difference when we walk our own path, relying on our strength, or when we invite Jesus to walk with us, leading us when we can no longer find a way.

All this month we will be reminded that even though there are hard times in this life, we are loved. We will be reminded that even though there are dark valleys and desperate times we can find the Hallelujahs.

So today, try to find a quiet space and listen. Listen for the Creator of the universe to speak to you and let you know you are His.

Dear Jesus,

Thank you for this day. Thank you for these words. Help me to find my strength in You. Help me to hear only Your voice and to know that I am enough. Help me to . . .

Weary

I'm tired of running.
I'm tired of trying.
I'm tired of crying.
I'm tired of being angry.
I'm tired of being afraid.
I'm tired of disappointing.
I'm tired of being tired.

I have been this tired. I have felt this alone. I have wanted to give up, and one summer evening I tried. But God rescued me. He shined His light on all the dark places of my life and made me brand new. I've had to learn to trust and return to Jesus each time I drifted away and remember with every fiber of my being that I am His.

What about you? Are you ready to surrender your life? Are you tired of running?

Dear Jesus,
Thank you for this day, . . . but I'm tired, Lord. I'm tired of being tired.
Help me to rest in You. Please forgive me for wanting to give up. Help
me to surrender my life. Help me to . . .

The Hard Days

Do you ever have one of those days? The ones where you wake up late, nothing goes right, you say all the wrong things, hear all the wrong things, live in the past, are afraid of the future, and before you know it it's time to go to bed and start it all over again the next day? Those are the days we need to pray the hardest. Those are also the days when we can learn the most.

I've found that during my worst days I've drawn the closest to God. I've truly leaned on Him, drawing His strength in my weak, insecure moments. And when I got through to the other side, there were lessons I learned that I would've never discovered if it had been a perfect day. In my thankfulness for the day being over, I find my gratefulness for what I learned, and if given a choice I would do that same day over again the exact same way.

Can you find the Hallelujah's in your hard days?

"Not only so, but we also glory in our sufferings, because we know that suffering produces perseverance; perseverance, character; and character, hope."
—ROMANS 5:3-4

"And we know that God in all things God works for the good or those who love him, who have been called according to his purpose. For those God foreknew he also predestined to be conformed to the image of his Son, that he might be the firstborn among many brothers and sisters."
—ROMANS 8:28-29

Dear Jesus,

Thank you for this day. Please help me in my hard days to search for You. Help me to . . .

Answered Prayer

I know there have been times in my life when I've questioned God and asked Him "Why aren't you answering my prayers?" At the time I didn't recognize my motives or the anger I was still holding onto or that I wasn't asking for God's will but for my own. I was still angry. I still thought God had forgotten me and forgotten His promises. It was in these moments that I pulled away from Him and started down a path of figuring out a way to answer my own prayers. If God wasn't going to, I would. And you can only imagine how that turned out. I made an even bigger mess and found myself a long way from the loving arms of my Father.

But slowly, carefully, He would speak to my heart and encourage me to return. I would either hear a song on the radio or talk to a friend or have someone tell me they were praying for me, and I would start the long walk back. He would welcome me with open arms and tell me that He missed me, and we would have a long conversation about what was best for me.

I encourage you today, if you're asking God this same question, to search your heart and surrender. Surrender your will. Surrender your personal desires. Surrender your doubt. Surrender your unforgiveness. Surrender your pride. Pray and ask God to give you a heart after His own, for His will to be done, and for His glory. You will find that if you do this God will answer your prayers perfectly—perfectly for you and in His perfect timing. Amen!

Dear Jesus,

Thank you for this day. Help me to trust You. Help me to remember that You have a perfect plan for my life. Help me to . . .

The Saddest Moments

What are my saddest moments? When I've slipped into the pit of complacency, discouragement, and dissatisfaction. My soul starts to sing a song that sounds like a bellow, looking at all the reasons I should be disappointed.

But I dig my hands into the dark, murky earth above me and crawl upward. I grab at whatever will hold me—rock and roots—and climb. I don't stop until I can see blue sky and feel the cool breeze on my cheeks and see the sunshine.

Don't ever give up, my friends. Don't live your life in sadness. It's exactly where the enemy wants you to be.

Cling to these verses while you're climbing upward:

"The LORD is close to the brokenhearted
    and saves those who are crushed in spirit."
—PSALM 34:18

"Cast your cares on the LORD
    and he will sustain you;
he will never let
    the righteous be shaken."
—PSALM 55:22

"Submit yourselves then, to God. Resist the devil, and he will flee from you."
—JAMES 4:7

Dear Jesus,
Thank you for this day. Help me to find my joy in You, Lord. Help me
in my sad moments. Help me to . . .

Psalm 8, a Psalm of David (1–8)

"LORD, our Lord,
    how majestic is your name in all the earth!

You have set your glory
    in the heavens.
Through the praise of children and infants
    you have established a stronghold against your enemies,
    to silence the foe and the avenger.
When I consider your heavens,
    the work of your fingers,
the moon and the stars,
    which you have set in place,
what is mankind that you are mindful of them,
    human beings that you care for them?

You have made them a little lower than the angels
    and have crowned them with glory and honor.
You made them rulers over the works of your hands;
    you put everything under their feet:
all flocks and herds,
    and the animals of the wild,
the birds in the sky,
    and the fish in the sea,
    all that swim the paths of the seas."

Dear Jesus,
Thank you for this day. Please help me in my hard days to see You. Help
me to . . .

Grief

Grief is definitely a hard and challenging thing we have to experience while living this life. The definition of grief is deep sorrow, especially when caused by someone's death. Grief synonyms include *misery, sadness, anguish, heartache, heartbreak, affliction,* and *mourning.* While grief typically relates to death itself, it is my experience that it's not only caused by the death of some*one* but by the death of some*thing.* It could be the death of a marriage, relationship, a season in your life, a job, or a dream. Whatever it is, grief comes in many shapes and sizes. Understanding grief and the rollercoaster of emotions it brings is like trying to predict a storm. But knowing who can calm the storm, the wind, and the waves, is what we need to hold onto. Jesus is the One who will get us through each painful moment and help us take the next step forward. He is our Hallelujah!

> "'Blessed are those who mourn,
>   for they will be comforted.'"
> —MATTHEW 5:4

Dear Jesus,
Thank you for this day. Please help me with my grief. Help me to find
my comfort in You. Help me to . . .

What Grief Is

At times we'd like to know there will be an end to our grief. Not forgetting about that person, not losing the love in our hearts, but letting go of the daily pain and sadness that we carry. But to do this we need to keep in mind what grief is and have the right perspective. Grief is:

- A natural response to pain and loss
- An emotional response that serves a purpose
- Temporary

Remember, too, that it's important in times of grief to tell God your feelings and share them with others. You may want to join a support group, ask people for specific prayer, or spend time with family and friends. We may want grief to work a certain way and have others understand what we're feeling, but what we don't always realize is that we need to trust God with our hearts and with His timing.

Dear Jesus,
Thank you for this day. Please help me with my grief. Help me to find my comfort in You. Help me to . . .

What Grief Does

My husband's first wife died of ovarian cancer almost 15 years ago. Over the years I've watched him grieve. Sometimes it's a faraway look. Sometimes it's a sadness that takes over the room. And sometimes it's a step backward into a world he wished he could have back. In these moments I also grieve. I grieve for their lost love. I grieve at his sadness. I grieve for myself and the insecurities that flood in when I know that I will never fill that void. Grief comes in many different forms. And every shape and size can be laid at Jesus' feet. When He wraps His arms around us, we know that this too shall pass and that someday "He will wipe every tear from their eyes. There will be no more death or mourning or crying or pain, for the old order of things has passed away" (Revelation 21:4).

I'm praying that today you will trust God with your grief. Let Him wrap His arms around you and give you peace.

Dear Jesus,
Thank you for this day. Please help me with my grief. Help me to find my comfort in You. Help me to . . .

Psalm 13, a Psalm of David

"How long, Lord? Will you forget me forever?
How long will you hide your face from me?
How long must I wrestle with my thoughts
and day after day have sorrow in my heart?
How long will my enemy triumph over me?

Look on me and answer, Lord my God.
Give light to my eyes, or I will sleep in death,
and my enemy will say, 'I have overcome him,'
and my foe will rejoice when I fall.

But I trust in your unfailing love;
my heart rejoices in your salvation.
I will sing the LORD's praise,
for he has been good to me."

Hallelujah! Thank you, Lord, that you never forget me, even when I feel alone. Help me to trust in you always, and remember all of your blessings. Amen.

Dear Jesus,

Thank you for this day. Thank you for these words. Help me to find my strength in You. Help me to . . .

Shattered

Have you ever walked into a plate glass window? I have a friend who describes it perfectly. You're walking along, she says, and everything is going great, when all of a sudden you hit something hard. You weren't expecting it and didn't see it coming.

I think this is the best way to describe the first year of my second marriage. I recently found something on Facebook that irrefutably explains my way of thinking that first year and why I hit so hard.

It's called the "Marriage Box." It talks about how most people who get married believe that marriage is going to be a box perpetually filled with all the things they've imagined. But the hard truth is that when we get married we start with an empty box. We need to put things in before we can take anything out.

When we got back from the honeymoon I opened the box. I was expecting to see all of these wonderful gifts that I was wanting this time around, but all I saw was the difficulty of moving to a new town, moving my kids into a home that had been shared by my new husband and his first wife, and feeling it had all been a lie.

I didn't blame God for this—I blamed myself. Even though I was finally developing a closer relationship with the Lord, I was still thinking that this marriage, this man, was going to fulfill me in all the ways my first marriage hadn't. And when I hit the glass, everything shattered. The truth is that only God can give you that kind of happiness; only God can fulfill you and give you true meaning in your life. Hallelujah!

Dear Jesus,
Thank you for this day. Help me to find my value in You. Help me to . . .

Praise in Prison

The letter to the Ephesians was written by Paul while he spent two years imprisoned in Rome. Can you imagine? When I try to, I don't see myself filled with the kind of joy and love that could produce what we read in the verses below:

> "Praise be to the God and Father of our Lord Jesus Christ, who has blessed us in the heavenly realms with every spiritual blessing in Christ. For he chose us in him before the creation of the world to be holy and blameless in his sight. In love he predestined us for adoption to sonship through Jesus Christ, in accordance with his pleasure and will—to the praise of his glorious grace, which he has freely given us in the One he loves. In him we have redemption through his blood, the forgiveness of sins, in accordance with the riches of God's grace that he lavished on us. With all wisdom and understanding, he made known to us the mystery of his will according to his good pleasure, which he purposed in Christ, to be put into effect when the times reach their fulfillment—to bring unity to all things in heaven and on earth under Christ."
> —EPHESIANS 1:3–10

It doesn't matter where we are at in this life—if we are filled with Christ, we have everything we need. I pray that you believe this today.

Dear Jesus,

Thank you for this day. Thank you for these words. Help me to find my strength in You. Help me to . . .

Psalm 20, a Psalm of David

"May the LORD answer you when you are in distress;
    may the name of the God of Jacob protect you.
May he send you help from the sanctuary
    and grant you support from Zion.
May he remember all your sacrifices
    and accept your burnt offerings.
May he give you the desire of your heart
    and make all your plans succeed.
May we shout for joy over your victory
    and lift up our banners in the name of our God.

May the LORD grant all your requests.

Now I know:
    The LORD gives victory to his anointed.
He answers him from his heavenly sanctuary
    with the victorious power of his right hand.
Some trust in chariots and some in horses,
    but we trust in the name of the LORD our God.
They are brought to their knees and fall,
    but we rise up and stand firm.
LORD, give victory to the king!
    Answer us when we call!"

Hallelujah! Thank you, Lord! Thank you for answering our prayers! Our trust is in You alone. We are victorious in You. Amen.

Dear Jesus,
Thank you for this day. Thank you for these words. Help me to find my strength in You. Help me to . . .

Never Stop Praying

In January 2011 we lost my grandmother to leukemia. She had battled hard for four years but on the morning of the thirtieth was taken up by angels to her heavenly home. She was a valiant prayer warrior and had prayed for each of her four children and her many grandchildren and great-grandchildren while she was here on earth.

On the day of the funeral, because I was the oldest I was pulled aside and presented with her Bible. While I had stayed strong throughout the days leading up to the funeral, I suddenly found myself with tears streaming down my face at the thought of this unbelievable gift.

She would read this Bible every morning and make small marks with pen near the verses that had touched her heart. At the bottom of each page there was clearly a worn mark where her thumb had grabbed the paper.

What a gift—not only the Bible but the memories that were passed along with it. Years of praying, reading, clutching His words until the very end. This was not only a Bible but a legacy I could carry on. I would pray for my family. I would read these words, just as Grandma did.

It didn't happen right away, but three years later I would be healed from my mental illness. I would go on to read this very Bible, every morning marking the pages in pen. God answered each of the countless prayers my grandma prayed for me over the years, and He continues to do so. Know this today: God answers prayers, in His timing and for His glory. If you're praying for someone today . . . , never give up.

Dear Jesus,

Thank you for this day. Thank you for the people who pray for me, and give me the strength to never give up praying for others. Help me to . . .

The First Move

Do you have a Thanksgiving tradition? A recipe that you have to make, or a game that you play as a family? Maybe you don't. Maybe Thanksgiving is hard, and there are no Hallelujahs for you. For me, Thanksgiving was a challenging day. For five years I had not spoken to my mom after a giant argument we'd had. Each of those five years, on Thanksgiving morning, I would wake up and start to prep the turkey to put in the oven. I would put on my apron and grab my "turkey" recipe card out of the box and hold it in my hand. In her handwriting it said, "Turkey-you can make." She had spelled out what I needed to do step by step, and I would remember when she first gave it to me. I missed her. I missed talking with her and laughing with her and regretted every word I had said. Year after year my heart hurt, until one year I snapped a picture of the card with my phone and texted her a note, saying "Happy Thanksgiving! Miss you Mom!" I didn't care if she didn't respond—it just felt so good to write those words and know she would read them.

It wasn't the first year, and not even the second, but eventually she responded. Eventually the texting became more frequent, and one day there was a call. We had made our way back to one another.

Sometimes you have to make the first move. Sometimes you have to swallow whatever pride you are holding onto and say "I'm sorry." The person has to be more important than the problem, . . . if you can even remember what the problem was. Forgiveness is freeing, and when you do it you will find your Hallelujah. Amen!

Dear Jesus,

Thank you for this day. Help me to forgive and let go. Help me to . . .

Stepping Into the Unknown

I love foggy mornings when the fields have this thin layer of cloud. The sunrise breaks through like shimmering diamonds, and it almost seems like another world. But foggy mornings remind me that we don't always know what the road ahead looks like. Sometimes seeing into the unknown can grip us with fear, and it feels like the safest thing to do is to turn around, because we know where we've been. But in Psalm 32:8 the Lord says, "I will instruct you and teach you in the way you should go; I will counsel you with my loving eye on you."

We don't always know the path ahead, but God does. Trust Him as you take one step at a time, into the unknown and into His care.

Dear Jesus,
Thank you for this day. Thank you for these words. Help me to find my strength in You. Help me to . . .

Psalm 27, a Psalm of David (1–5)

"The LORD is my light and my salvation—
    whom shall I fear?
The LORD is the stronghold of my life—
    of whom shall I be afraid?

When the wicked advance against me
        to devour me,
it is my enemies and my foes
        who will stumble and fall.
Though an army besiege me,
        my heart will not fear;
though war break out against me,
        even then will I be confident.

One thing I ask from the LORD,
        this is what I seek:
that I may dwell in the house of the LORD
        all the days of my life,
to gaze upon the beauty of the LORD
        and to seek him in his temple.
For in the day of trouble
        he will keep me safe in his dwelling;
he will hide me in the shelter of his sacred tent
        and set me high upon a rock."

Dear Jesus,
Thank you for this day. Thank you for these words. Teach me Your ways
and help me to wait on You. Help me to . . .

The Battle Is Real

I don't know about you, but there are times when I feel I'm living in a war zone. There are days when I'm dodging bullets of discouragement, arrows of sadness, nets of lies . . . and I've had it! The battle is real, my friends. The enemy will not take my happiness, my freedom, my pursuit of the kingdom of God, and you should not let him take yours.

I've started reading a book titled *The Invisible War* by Chip Ingram. I wanted to share part of it with you today: "Jesus knew the battle was real. When he was in agony in the Garden of Gethsemane the night before his crucifixion, he was tempted to quit. When life got hard, he never put on a superhero cape and forgot about being a man. He was fully God, but he was also fully man, and the Bible tells us he was tempted with lust, with anger, with depression, with envy, and with a false belief that people probably wouldn't accept his sacrifice, so why bother: He agonized to the point of sweating drops of blood. What did Jesus do to overcome this battle? He prayed. His three closest friends were there with him, and the one thing he asked them to do was to pray."

Besides praying, Chip Ingram also says we need to "allow ourselves to be continually strengthened by the power already available to us in our relationship with Christ. This is the same power that raised Jesus from the dead and now dwells in us."

Do you believe that? Because that is what we need to do: pray for ourselves, for our families, and for each other and have faith in the power of Jesus Christ! I hope you will stand with me as we fight this battle! Amen!

Dear Jesus,

Thank you for this day. Help me to put on the full armor of Christ and battle in Your name. Help me to . . .

Wake Up

When Jesus was on the Mount of Olives, before his enemies came to arrest Him, He asked the disciples to pray. "When he rose from prayer and went back to the disciples, he found them asleep, exhausted from sorrow. 'Why are you sleeping?' he asked them. 'Get up and pray so that you will not fall into temptation.'" (Luke 22:46).

Brothers and sisters, it's time to wake up! It's time to rise up and pray. Rise up and pray for our country. Rise up and pray for our leaders. Rise up and pray for the communities in which we live. Rise up and pray for our family and children. Rise up and pray for wisdom, and that we will not listen to the lies of the enemy.

There will be moments in this life when we will question—we'll question why it has to be this hard, why we are here, how long it will have to be this way. But we need to remember that God never promised this life would be easy—only that He would never leave us nor forsake us. He is refining us with fire so that we can someday stand on streets of gold. So rise up and remember that God is still in control—we already know how this story ends! Amen.

Dear Jesus,
Thank you for this day. Thank you for these words. Help me to rise up
and pray. Help me to . . .

Our "To-Do" List

I know there's a lot to do: deadlines at work, groceries to buy, bills to pay, school sports, errands to run, doctor appointments . . . the list can go on and on. And *everyone* I talk to says how unbelievably busy they are. After church one Sunday it was the same conversation over and over again. I myself feel the weight of my "to-do" list and look around and see how we worriedly move through each day—fast-paced, list in hand, trying to get caught up. But what if this were just another way to separate us from God? Another lie from the enemy that we need to always be on the go, swimming against the current to stay afloat?

When I think about this, I'm reminded of the story in Luke 10 about Mary and Martha:

> "As Jesus and his disciples were on their way, he came to a village where a woman named Martha opened her home to him. She had a sister called Mary, who sat at the Lord's feet listening to what he said. But Martha was distracted by all the preparations that had to be made. She came to him and asked, 'Lord, don't you care that my sister has left me to do the work by myself? Tell her to help me!' 'Martha, Martha,' the Lord answered, 'you are worried and upset about many things, but few things are needed—or indeed only one. Mary has chosen what is better, and it will not be taken from her.'"
> —LUKE 10:38–42

When you read this, what do you suppose the "one thing" is? I believe it is our relationship with Jesus Christ. When we focus on this, everything else will fall into place.

Dear Jesus,
Thank you for this day. Help me to have a heart like Mary's, wanting to sit at Your feet and worship You. Help me to . . .

The Impossible Mountain

In February 2017 we moved my mom in to live with us. Yes, the same woman I hadn't spoken to in five years. She'd had two heart attacks and two strokes within a two-year time frame and was at the point where she could no longer drive, work, or afford to live on her own.

I flew to Tucson, Arizona, after work on the 24th; arrived at the airport around midnight; was picked up by a mutual friend and dropped off at my mom's condo; slept a couple hours; and was back at the airport the next morning for the first flight back to Michigan. It was a whirlwind trip, but God was so faithful. He walked with me every step of the way and gave me the strength I needed. It was hard, but the Hallelujahs rang across the country as I brought her home to live with us.

I'm not sure what you're going through today, but you need to know this: no matter what it is, God is walking with you. He will give you the strength you need for whatever mountain you think may be impossible to climb, and from the top take the time to show you the incredible view. Hallelujah!

Dear Jesus,
Thank you for this day. Thank you for walking with me. Help me to . . .

Psalm 30, a Psalm of David (1–2, 6–12)

"I will exalt you, LORD,
    for you lifted me out of the depths
    and did not let my enemies gloat over me.
LORD my God, I called to you for help,
    and you healed me. . . .

When I felt secure, I said,
    'I will never be shaken.'
LORD, when you favored me,
    you made my royal mountain stand firm;
but when you hid your face,
    I was dismayed.

To you, LORD, I called;
    to the LORD I cried for mercy:
'What is gained if I am silenced,
    if I go down to the pit?
Will the dust praise you?
    Will it proclaim your faithfulness?
Hear, LORD, and be merciful to me;
    LORD, be my help.'

You turned my wailing into dancing;
    you removed my sackcloth and clothed me with joy,
that my heart may sing your praises and not be silent.
    LORD my God, I will give you thanks forever."

Dear Jesus,
Thank you for this day. Thank you for these words. Help me to . . .

A Prayer for You

I'm always on the lookout for prayers. Prayers that I can read and share with the For His Glory community. When I came across this one, I definitely wanted to share it with you. I pray that it will be a blessing today.

Heavenly Father, you are good.
May Your Kingdom be our only motive,
the gospel be our only aim,
and Your love be our only anthem.
Thank you for unconditionally, perfectly, and consistently
loving us for all
we have been, all we are, and all we have yet to become.
May we learn to love like you love.
Let our perspectives be gained in the light of eternity.
May our hearts be soft and teachable. May we be people of
intentionality.
Thank you for hemming us in behind and before; for
laying your hand upon us.
May we be sensitive to your Holy Spirit; never walking
away from your voice,
content to settle for nothing less than radical obedience.
Teach us to trust you with complete abandon.

Amen.

(USED WITH PERMISSION FROM R. ATTEMA)

Dear Jesus,
Thank you for this day. Thank you for these words. Help me to . . .

Wait for the Lord

My friends, it may sometimes feel like it's the end of the road. That there is darkness all around you and you have no more strength to fight. But the Bible says that "those who hope in the LORD will renew their strength. They will soar on wings like eagles; they will run and not grow weary, they will walk and not be faint" (Isaiah 40:31).

Remember, God goes before us and will fight for us! Wait for the Lord, and keep the faith!

Dear Jesus,

Thank you for this day. Thank you for the breath in my lungs and for waking me up this morning. I believe that You are my strength. I believe that You are my truth. Help me lean into You in my weak moments. Help me not to listen to the lies of the enemy. Guard me with Your angels and protect me from the evil one. Help me to live this day confident that You go before me. I pray this for myself, for my loved ones, for every person who is reading this today, and for their family and friends. I love You and praise You and ask these things in Your precious name, Amen.

Dear Jesus,

Thank you for this day. Help me to remember that You go before me and will fight for me. Help me to . . .

Breathe today. Not have a
pani attack today driving to
Skywood c Julie! So scared,
as close to as scared as I have
ever been. Help me walk through
the doors + receive help.
Help me surrender to you +
your will. Please hold my
hand and heart. Amen

He Is in the Waiting

Take courage, my friends. He is with you in the waiting room, in the diagnosis, in the unemployment line, in the counseling office, and at the dining table when there is no food, no hope, no electricity. He is with you at the first breath, at the last, walking down the aisle, walking to the courthouse, standing at a church pew, or behind bars. He loves you, died for you, and came to give you hope and a future. He is with you in all of these things and more. He is even with you in the waiting . . .

Precious Jesus,
My hope is in You, Lord, even when everything around me feels like it's out of control. You know what I need before I even ask, and You can see much farther down the road than I can from Your heavenly vantage point. Please help me to trust You, and give me patience in the waiting. Amen.

Dear Jesus,
Thank you for this day. Help me to take courage in the waiting. Help me to . . .

Survive my real first day here. Be open + honest. Hold me.

Psalm 34, a Psalm of David (1–10, 15)

I will extol the LORD at all times;
    his praise will always be on my lips.
I will glory in the LORD;
    let the afflicted hear and rejoice.
Glorify the LORD with me;
    let us exalt his name together.

I sought the LORD, and he answered me;
    he delivered me from all my fears.
Those who look to him are radiant;
    their faces are never covered with shame.
This poor man called, and the LORD heard him;
    he saved him out of all his troubles.
The angel of the LORD encamps around those who fear him,
    and he delivers them.

Taste and see that the LORD is good;
    blessed is the one who takes refuge in him.
Fear the LORD, you his holy people,
    for those who fear him lack nothing.
The lions may grow weak and hungry,
    but those who seek the LORD lack no good thing. . . .

The eyes of the LORD are on the righteous.
    and his ears are attentive to their cry."

Dear Jesus,

Thank you for this day. Thank you for these words. Help me to . . .

listen, learn, heal

The Book of Job

We can't move through this month without talking about Job. In my NIV Bible before the first chapter begins, the Introduction states, "The book of Job questions the reasons for suffering, especially the suffering of people who love God and are good. Job's friends insisted that he was suffering as punishment for his sin. Job defended himself by insisting that he had done nothing seriously wrong and then expressed his trust in God."

But what I love about Job is that the book makes me question my faith. Could I endure all of the things that Job went through, including losing all of his flocks, his personal wealth, his family, and his health, all in a short period of time, and still praise God? Could I be put to the test and still proclaim my Hallelujahs?

And while Job and his friends go back and forth, giving their reasoning behind Job's hardships, talking of God as though they understand why He does the things He does, the Lord speaks: "Who is this that obscures my plans with words without knowledge? Brace yourself like a man; I will question you, and you shall answer me. Where were you when I laid the earth's foundation? Tell me, if you understand. Who marked off its dimensions? Surely you know! Who stretched a measuring line across it? On what were its footings set, or who laid the cornerstone—while the morning stars sang together and all the angels shouted for joy?" (Job 38:2–7).

I read these words and realize that God is more than I can fathom or imagine. While I can pretend to know why things happen the way they do, I will never know God's plan or His reasons. It is in the hard times that I can only trust God's Word and know that His ways are higher than mine. His love is greater than mine. His will is more perfect than mine. Hallelujah! Praise His holy name!

Dear Jesus,

Thank you for this day. Help me to trust You and praise You in the hard times. Help me to . . . Trust you and your timing. Write off my family + friends -

Choose Joy

As I mentioned earlier this month, we moved my mom in to live with us in February 2017. While it was a blessing to see her every day after going so long without any correspondence, it was challenging to see what the heart attacks and strokes had done. This vibrant woman who had run up to seven miles a day and had driven all over the Western United States now walked with a cane, and I drove her for shopping and to her appointments. I could have questioned God about what had happened and how her life had changed so abruptly. But it was easy to see that He was walking with her and that she was no longer relying on her own independence but leaning into the precious arms of Jesus for her every need.

There are moments when she wishes she could go back—back to life the way it was before. But my mom has realized that this life is only temporary and that without these physical impairments she's not sure she would have slowed down enough to see who God really is. In these hard moments she chooses joy and triumphantly yells her Hallelujahs through the pain, through the frustration, through the heartache, and knows she would rather be here and on the doorstep of heaven than anywhere else in this world.

Today, I encourage you to know that whatever you are going through God has a perfect plan for your life if you will only trust Him. You might not be able to see it now, but if you rest in Him, you will.

Dear Jesus,

Thank you for this day. Help me to trust You and praise You in the hard times. Help me to . . .

The Cup

When I look through the Bible and scan every page, there is no greater example of suffering with obedience and joy than that of our Savior Jesus Christ. He knew that He would suffer and die for our sins, yet He continued to walk toward the cross without hesitation and leaned into His Father for wisdom and direction. He fell to the ground in the garden and prayed earnestly, dripping blood and overwhelmed with sorrow: "'My Father, if it is possible, may this cup be taken from me. Yet not as I will, but as you will'" (Matthew 26:39).

And when the answer was no—that Jesus would need to drink the cup for all humankind—he stood up and reached out for it with both hands. He wasn't dragged, kicking and screaming. He wasn't angry with His Father. He didn't pull away from His Father's love.

How many times have I cried "Take this from me, Lord!"? How many times have I asked the question *Why*? How many times have I distanced myself from God because I was angry and no longer wanted the cup that was before me? Too many to count. If I could pray only one prayer, it would be that I could walk wherever God asks me to go, regardless of the struggles that I may endure, and be faithful and obedient in the journey, no matter the cost.

What about you? Are you going through something right now that you would like to run from? What would it look like for you to stand firm and reach out for the cup?

Dear Jesus,

Thank you for this day. Help me to walk wherever You ask me to go.
Help me to . . .

When We're Tempted to Stay

Have you ever been tempted? Whatever the temptation, it's never easy, but what if you know you need to move on from a situation and you're tempted to stay? Staying means accepting that things will stay the same, no matter how unhealthy they are. Staying means you're willing to keep enduring whatever pain you're experiencing. Staying sometimes seems easier than the unknown.

If this is you today, I would encourage you to pray through the temptation. Beth Moore writes in her book *To Live Is Christ—Day by Day*, "Paul's actions teach us an important lesson. We obviously need to avoid temptation, but when we can't help but face it, we can prepare ourselves."

What does "preparing" ourselves look like? We can pray in advance and ask Jesus to give us wisdom. We can pray and ask Him to give us courage. We can pray and ask Jesus to go before us and prepare the way. Whatever the temptation, even if it's to stay in an unhealthy and hard situation, Jesus will walk with us every step of the way, out into freedom, where we can joyfully say Hallelujah!

All this month we were reminded that even though there are hard things in this life, we are loved. And even when we walk through the dark valleys and desperate times, we know that Jesus is walking with us. We know He will help us, and we can find our Hallelujahs.

Dear Jesus,

Thank you for being the example I need to follow. Please give me the strength I need to stand up and walk the road that is before me. Help me to be obedient in all things and know that You have a plan for my life. Help me to sing Hallelujah in the hard times and know that You are walking with me. In Your precious name I pray these things, Amen.

Dear Jesus,

Thank you for this day. Help me, Lord, to . . . listen + be willing + Do your will not mine.

October

CONVERSATIONS WITH GOD

*"If my people, who are called by
my name, will humble themselves and pray
and seek my face and turn from their wicked
ways, then I will hear from heaven, and I will
forgive their sin and will heal their land."*

—2 CHRONICLES 7:14

An Amazing Journey

Is it sometimes hard to pray? Is it hard to find the words to talk with someone you cannot see and who feels a million miles away? First of all, don't believe the lie. The enemy will tell you anything to keep you from talking to God. "You don't have time this morning." "What will you say?" "Do you really think He hears your prayers?" "You are not worthy to talk with Jesus."

These lies couldn't be further from the truth. Jesus is not asking for lengthy, drawn out prayers with big words. He wants our praise, our concerns, and our needs, and He wants to have a relationship with us. A prayer can be as easy as breathing out "Thank you!" and as meaningful as saying "I love you, Lord."

All this month we are going to work on our conversations with God. Each day there will a prayer to pray aloud, or a prompt, or questions to answer. Writing out our prayers is a powerful way to communicate with God, and a way that we can look back and see how He has answered our prayers. So breath in and exhale all the lies, all the preconceived notions, and all the things you've thought about prayer, and get ready to start an amazing journey . . .

Father God, Lord Jesus, Holy Spirit,
I pray for a refreshed awareness of You this month. I pray that we can feel You sitting next to us, talking to us as a friend. I rebuke the enemy's lies and pray that we will know in our hearts that Your deepest desire is to be in relationship with us. We love You, Lord, and look forward to all that You are going to do. Amen.

Dear Jesus,
Thank you for this day! Help me to stop listening to the lies of the enemy and believing it's hard to pray. Help me to tell You my concerns, my needs, and my praise. Help me to . . .

Praise

Today's devotional prompt:

We start with praise! There is so much to be thankful for. Count up all the things you're thankful for and write them down. Thank Him for a situation you just came through or a new season you are starting. Praise Him for loving you and let Him know how you feel.

Dear Jesus,

Thank you for knowing me better than anyone else. You know exactly what I need before I even ask, and Your love heals my hurts in ways I cannot even comprehend. Your gifts are extravagant, and Your beauty is all around me. I love You, and I offer my whole self as a living sacrifice for Your glory. Thank you for today! Thank you for . . .

Struggles

Today's devotional prompt:

I'm struggling today, Lord. You've promised to never leave me nor forsake me, yet I feel all alone. Remind me today of who You are and what I need. Help me to feel You in a real and tangible way. I need Your help today.

Dear Jesus,
Thank you for walking with me: even when the water gets deep, even when the waves crash against me, even when I'm in over my head. You are faithful, Lord, and I will trust You. Help me to . . .

Fears

Today's devotional prompt:

Is there something you're afraid of? Tell God your fears and then let them go . . .

Dear Jesus,
I'm afraid today. I've been listening to the lies of the enemy and I cannot let them go. Help me as I write them down and put them into Your light. I'm afraid of . . .

Addictions

Today's devotional prompt:

Statistics say that over 20 million people (in the United States alone) suffer from drug and alcohol abuse issues. Perry Stone, international evangelist and author of There's a Crack in Your Armor, has spoken to literally hundreds of men and women who have battled addictions and are now free. He writes: "When asking them, why they turned to drugs and alcohol, about nine out of ten gave me the same answer. They replied, 'I did it to dull the pain and the hurts I was feeling in my life.' After hearing this response over and over for many years, I then saw another aspect of Satan's strategy. By keeping a person high or drunk, the enemy is also dulling them to the point where they cannot feel the joy and peace that comes from the presence of God."

If this is you, battling an addiction right now . . . there is hope! Find an accountability group and attend meetings. But also recognize the battle and who it is you are fighting. Today, admit to the Lord what you're addicted to, and tell Him you need His help.

Dear Jesus,
I cry out to You this morning with a loud voice. Help me . . .

Letting Go

Today's devotional prompt:

Is there something you've been keeping from God? Be honest with Him today and write down what you've been holding onto. There is complete freedom in repenting and receiving His forgiveness . . .

Dear Jesus,

Forgive me, Lord, for keeping from You that . . .

The Fence

Today's devotional prompt:

Help me, Lord, to not get pulled into this world. Help me to let go of the illusions and believe in You. I'm walking the fence between this world and You, and I'm tired of the lies. Help me today to lay it all down at Your feet.

Dear Jesus,
Please hear my prayer and have mercy on me. I have strayed from You and Your voice, and the voices I hear now confuse me and I don't know what to do. Please help me . . .

Choose to Be Thankful

Today's devotional prompt:

No matter what you're going through today, choose to be thankful. Identify all of the things that you are thankful for, and let Him know by jotting down your list, below . . .

Dear Jesus,
Thank you for . . .

Petitions and Requests

Today's devotional prompt:

Are there specific prayers your family or friends need? Write them down below. Offer up your prayers today . . .

Dear Jesus,
I lift up my family to you. I pray specifically for . . .

Thanksgiving

Today's devotional prompt:

Center your conversation with God today on this prayer from Psalm 30:11–12:

> Lord God,
> "You did it: You turned my deepest pains into joyful dancing;
> > You stripped off my dark clothing
> > and covered me with joyful light.
> You have restored my honor. My heart is ready to explode, erupt
> > in new songs!
> > It's impossible to keep quiet!
> > Eternal One, my God, my Life-giver, I will thank You forever"
> (VOICE).
> —PSALM 30:11–12

Dear Jesus,
Thank you for Your amazing gifts! Thank you for . . .

Day I left Skywood 2020

I'm Fine

Today's devotional prompt:

I'm still saying "I'm fine," Lord. I'm still prentending that I have it all together. Help me to reach out to someone today and share my struggles. Help me to be vulnerable if someone asks how I'm really doing. Bring me someone trustworthy, Lord.

Dear Jesus,

I have joy because I know You are working in my heart to make me more like You. Help me to live in community. Help me so that what I'm going through can help others. Help me to . . .

The Small Stuff

Today's devotional prompt:

Write out all of the "small stuff" that's on your mind today. Did you lose your keys? What are you axious about? Do you have to get groceries and are worried about your budget? Do you have a big meeting that you're nervous about? Do you have a cold? Write it down and give it over to the Lord.

Dear Jesus,
Forgive me for the times I don't talk with You about the "small stuff"—
the things I think You're too busy for. Today I need help with . . .

He Loves Me Anyway

Today's devotional prompt:

I have great joy today because the Lord sees me for who I really am, . . . and loves me anyway. I cannot fool Him. Even though I put on clothes and present to the world my best self, despite the fact that I'm struggling inside, they do not see my pain. But my God does. And He goes before me and holds my hand. I am grateful.

Dear Jesus,
Thank you that You see me for who I really am. Today, in spite of what I show my family and friends, I'm struggling with . . .

Why Did Jesus Cross the Lake?

Today's devotional prompt:

Today, read Mark 5:1–20. When you're done, ask yourself this question: Why did Jesus go across the lake in the first place?

You see, God sent Jesus into the world to save us! He is our lifeline, and if we follow Him He'll show us how to walk this earth and prepare us for our heavenly home. If you believe this and choose to follow Him, no matter what the enemy does to you it will not stop Jesus from getting to you. He'll cross the lake just for you every time.

Dear Jesus,

Thank you for loving me. Thank you for finding me and helping me. Today, help me to . . .

The Noise of this World

Today's devotional prompt:

Please help me when I let the noises of this world drown out the sound of Your voice. I am guilty of being too busy, too preoccupied, too eager to do other things rather than spending time with You. I admit that I have not totally surrendered my entire life to You. I am selfish and hold things back that I still want to enjoy, even when I know they're wrong in Your eyes. Forgive me, Lord.

Dear Jesus,
Help me. Train my ears to hear Your voice. Help me to prioritize my day and keep You first. Help me to . . .

Search Your Heart

Today's devotional prompt:

The word that best describes the emotion in my heart today is . . .

Dear Jesus,

. . .

Finding Your Joy

Today's devotional prompt:

Today I have joy, because I know You are working in my heart to make me stronger and helping me work through my issue with . . .

Dear Jesus,
Please continue to give me strength on this journey. Help me to . . .

The Leaking Pen

Today's devotional prompt:

Yesterday I struggled with a leaking pen. I couldn't figure out which pen it was, since every time I grabbed for a different one small bits of black ink ended up on my hand. I finally pulled out all of the pens and noticed ink at the bottom of the holder. One pen had leaked, but now every pen that was in the jar had touched the ink and was stained. I had it on my hands, my desk, everywhere.

I was suddenly reminded that this was like the sin in our lives. When we allow a little in, it starts to spread to other areas, and before we know it it's touching everything. Realizing this, I was grateful that Jesus doesn't throw us away, as I did the jar. When we ask for forgiveness, He washes us white as snow, and the stains are gone.

Today, take an inventory of your life and make sure there are no leaky pens. If there are, invite Jesus to wash over you with His forgiveness and give you clean hands and a pure heart.

Dear Jesus,
Search my heart. Make me aware of any sin in my life. Help me to . . .

The Lies

Today's devotional prompt:

I'm not sure why we believe the lies. Maybe because they come so quickly, like flaming arrows that penetrate our heart. But you need to cry out loud and speak the name of Jesus. Let His name be on your lips today. Tell Him what you're feeling and what lies you believe.

Dear Jesus,
I cry out to you this morning with a loud voice. Forgive me that I get so easily discouraged. Let me hear Your truth today. I'm tired of the lies I so often hear, like . . .

What Is Your Weakness?

Today's devotional prompt:

What is your weakness? For me, the enemy used depression to make me forget who I was in Christ. For years I struggled with mental illness, and the one constant theme in all of his lies was that I would never get better. I heard "God can't heal you," "He doesn't care," "It wouldn't matter if you died." But God *did* heal me, my friend! He does care! And it does matter that you're here, too! You have been created by God, in His image and for His glory, and he has great plans for you.

Today, write down your weakness, what the enemy uses against you, and replace it with God's truth!

Dear Jesus,

There are days I struggle, but not today. Today I'm reminded that Satan uses my weaknesses against me. But today I choose Your truth. Today I choose to believe that . . .

To-Do List

Today's devotional prompt:

Today, look at your to-do list. For each item, ask yourself why it is that on the list. Are there things that can be eliminated or postponed? Are they important? Anxiety is not of God but from the enemy. Remember that when you're anxious and stressed, worrying about what's before you, you are missing out on God's peace.

Dear Jesus,

Remind me today that you are in control of all things. I feel overwhelmed with to-do my list, what's before me, and everything that is going on. Help me to feel Your presence today. Please go before me and . . .

Doors

Today's devotional prompt:

Yesterday was a day about doors. Not only did we talk about doors in church, but my husband and I went for a motorcycle ride and ended up driving by the farmhouse I grew up in. If you've read my story, you'll know that this was only one address out of many I had while growing up, but it was definitely one of the important ones for me. I was reminded of the many doors I've walked through, the ones I've pulled shut, and the doors that I see coming on this journey. The beautiful thing is that Jesus has been there for every door, even the ones I've forced my way through and should have never opened.

Today, if you are coming to an unopened door, listen for His voice, be in His Word, and be obedient if you need either to go through or to resist that temptation.

Dear Jesus,
Help me to listen for Your voice today. Help me to . . .

To Be Humble

Today's devotional prompt:

> "'The greatest among you will be your servant. For those who exalt themselves will be humbled, and those who humble themselves will be exalted.'"
> —MATTHEW 23:11-12

Write out below what this verse means to you . . .

Dear Jesus,
Thank you for being the ultimate example of a servant. Help me to . . .

Be Still and Know

Today's devotional prompt:

Take time today to be still. Turn off the TV and radio, find a peaceful space, quiet your mind, and just focus on God. Let His peace rush in to replace the noise of this world.

Dear Jesus,
Thank you for this quiet time. Thank you that I'm able to just sit here and enjoy my time with You. Help me . . .

God Is Love

Today's devotional prompt:

How do we respond to a broken and hurting world? Not with violence or anger or harsh words or nasty emails or cruel Facebook posts, but with love. God *is* love! Is there someone today who needs your love? Search your heart and do something special for that someone today.

Dear Jesus,
Help me to love like You. Help me to . . .

A Slow Fade

Today's devotional prompt:

Lord,
I admit to You today that I've stepped off Your path. Help me to do more than
simply go through the motions of worship and service. Create in me a heart
that hungers for You alone.

Dear Jesus,
I come before You today to let You know that I don't like the backward
steps I take. I don't like it when I don't trust You and when I doubt
You're listening. Is that when I'm listening to voices other than Yours? I
pray, Lord, that You will help me through this. Help me to be confident
in You. Help me to . . .

10,005 minutes

Today's devotional prompt:

There are 10,005 minutes in a week. Write down some of the things you would like to do in the coming week. What are some spiritual goals you would like to make for yourself?

Dear Jesus,
Thank you for time. Help me to use it wisely and prioritize what I need to do. Help me to . . .

Answered Prayer

Today's devotional prompt:

Do you believe in answered prayer? I do, but I didn't understand the full extent of one of His answers until I sat at my father-in-law's funeral. God didn't take lightly my prayer to find a man who believed in God and loved Him. He answered it for me, for my children, and for my children's children. The answer came not only in the form of a man, but in his family, and in how a legacy would continue to be passed down to many generations. I tell you this today because if you are waiting for an answered prayer, keep waiting until God delivers it to you in His timing. It will be the most perfect answer, one that will not only touch your life but the lives of those around you.

What answer to prayer are you waiting for today?

Dear Jesus,
Thank you for answered prayer! Today, I pray for . . .

Are You Tired?

Today's devotional prompt:

Are you tired of listening to the enemy's lies? Tired of him questioning your identity in Christ? Tired of him stealing your joy? Then arm yourself with the truth! Rebuke the enemy and call on the name of Jesus! Tell Jesus what you're struggling with today and bring it out into His light . . .

Dear Jesus,
I lay before You today these lies, to replace with Your truth. Help me to . . .

The Bible

Today's devotional prompt:

We don't get to pick and choose what we like or don't like in the Bible. Second Timothy 3:16–17 says, "All Scripture is God-breathed and is useful for teaching, rebuking, correcting and training in righteousness, so that the servant of God may be thoroughly equipped for every good work."

Today, ask God to open your eyes to His truth. Let the Bible become your manual for living and a way to hear from your heavenly Father.

Dear Jesus,
Thank you for Your Word. Help me to . . .

Reflection

Today's devotional prompt:

Lord,
Am I as pure a reflection of You as I can be? Am I walking in Your shadow and trusting You with my life? Am I living for You, or for the people around me? Am I being obedient to all You ask of me? Lord, You know my heart. Reveal to me the things I need to do to be more like You.

Dear Jesus,
Help me to live intentionally. Empty me of all the things that are of me and fill me with You. Help me today to . . .

Continuing the Journey

I hope you have enjoyed this month's intentional devotional approach, and I hope you've enjoyed spending time each day with God in prayer. My prayer for you moving forward is that you will continue. I pray that you'll be able to exhale all the lies, set aside all of the excuses, open up your schedule, and make a way to spend time each day fully immersed in the presence of God.

And keep in mind that there are many ways to pray. If journaling is not for you, spend time praying while you're driving in your car. Take moments to praise Him when on a break at work or taking a walk in His beautiful creation. Find moments throughout your day to just whisper "Thank you, Lord" and "I love You."

J. C. Ryle writes, "Faith is to the soul what life is to the body. Prayer is to faith what breath is to the body." So make your prayer life as important and as automatic as taking a breath. And never give up. Life will always be busy, and the enemy will always find ways to keep you from this. But never stop finding a way to spend time with your Lord. Amen.

Dear Jesus,

Thank you for this day. Thank you for this past month and the time I spent with You. I don't want it to end. Help me to . . .

November

THANKFUL

"Give thanks in all circumstances;
for this is God's will for you
in Christ Jesus."

–1 THESSALONIANS 5:18

To Be Truly Thankful

November is one of my favorite months. I love the earthtone colors, the way everything has quieted down after the busyness of summer, putting a sweater on and going for a walk, and the act of Thanksgiving. For me, it's not only about the food and the fellowship with family but a way to physically celebrate and share with others the gratefulness in my heart.

All of this month we are going to reflect on what it looks like to be truly thankful. We'll look at verses, things we can do to show how thankful we are, and prayers we can pray. The Bible tells us that gratitude is not only a feeling but a way of life, and I'm excited to look closer at this with you.

> "Let the message of Christ dwell among you richly as you teach and admonish one another with all wisdom through psalms, hymns, and songs from the Spirit, singing to God with gratitude in your hearts. And whatever you do, whether in word or deed, do it all in the name of the Lord Jesus, giving thanks to God the Father through him."
> —COLOSSIANS 3:16–17

Dear Jesus,
Thank you for this day. Thank you for everything that I have, for I know it comes from You. Help me to have a thankful heart. Help me to . . .

Definition of Thankful

What does thankfulness mean to you? The Merriam Webster's dictionary describes "thankful" as: conscious of the benefit received, expressive of thanks, and well pleased. The Bible tells us in 1 Thessalonians 5:18 to "give thanks in all circumstances, for this is God's will for you in Christ Jesus."

So, what does this mean? I've included some principles, below. Reflect on each letter and phrase and think about what being thankful means to you.

Teach others to be grateful.

Humble yourself before the Lord.

Always thank the Lord.

Never take His gifts for granted.

Know that all we have are gifts from Him.

Find the blessing.

Use your gifts to help others.

Love in all that you do.

Dear Jesus,

Thank you for this day. Teach me to be thankful in all circumstances.
Help me to . . .

Teach Others to Be Grateful

Have you ever taught someone to be thankful? When my children were little, I would tell them to say the words "thank you." I would encourage them to use these words after receiving a gift or something they had asked for. But when they're young, it's hard to convey why we're saying the words. It's also hard to explain a grateful heart.

Still, from a young age saying "thank you" can become a habit. We may say the words automatically, perhaps never fully understanding or contemplating the gift or act or what it truly cost the giver.

I don't think I fully understood what it meant to be grateful until I was in my thirties. I had gone through most of my life expecting and believing I could make things happen. But when things started to fall apart around me, and there was no more magic in my bag to pull out, I realized that control is an illusion and that my greatest blessings didn't happen because of me; they were gifts from God. I could finally see these gifts and what they truly cost Him, and gratitude filled my heart.

Can we teach others to be thankful? I think we can prepare the way. I think it's important to teach the words, as well as the meaning behind them. I think we can model gratefulness in our own lives and tell others why we have it. But the greatest gift we were ever given was Jesus Christ and what He did for us on the cross. Until you receive that gift, "thank you" will just be empty words.

Dear Jesus,

Thank you for this day. Teach me to model gratitude to others. Help me share Your good news. Help me to . . .

Humble Yourself Before the Lord

In 2007 I was laid off, and so was my ex-husband. The money he had been giving me stopped, and unemployment took forever to come. I had two children to take care of and no idea how I would buy food or pay my bills. For so long I had relied on myself to make a way, and now I stood with my hands in the air, turning over my situation to God and having to trust that He would provide our every need. I humbled myself before the Lord and admitted I could not do this without Him. I would have to be patient and allow Him to make a way.

One night there was a knock at the door, and a youth group stopped by with bags of groceries. I was overwhelmed. How could they have known? But it was God. He knew my every need and provided us not only with food but with people who helped with my bills and then later with a new job.

People stepped up, acting as the hands and feet of Jesus, and I was thankful. Thankful when I stood in line at the food pantry, thankful that I had a warm house, thankful that he met every need and paid every bill. There was always something to be thankful for, and I carry that gratefulness with me today.

Do you believe He will provide for you? Today, humble yourself before the Lord and admit that you need Him; admit that you can't do this life without Him.

Dear Jesus,

Thank you for this day. Humble me, Lord. Help me to trust You with all things. Help me to . . .

Always Thank the Lord

Sometimes it's easy to focus on all the things that go wrong in our lives. We can get stuck on the bad days, the painful seasons, the challenging roads, and lose sight of the other gifts that are coming right at the same time.

Paul says in Philippians 4:4–7, "Rejoice in the Lord always. I will say it again: Rejoice! Let your gentleness be evident to all. The Lord is near. Do not be anxious about anything, but in every situation, by prayer and petition, with thanksgiving, present your requests to God. And the peace of God, which transcends all understanding, will guard your hearts and your minds in Christ Jesus."

So how about today, as we think about all the things we have to be thankful for? Make a list, say them out loud, concentrate on all the good gifts, and praise our Savior for them. Rejoice in the Lord! He is a good, good Father . . . today and every day, and we need to let Him know we recognize and appreciate it. Always thank the Lord.

Dear Jesus,

Thank you for this day. Thank you for walking with me and for every good gift. I praise You today! I rejoice in . . .

Never Take His Gifts for Granted

"A good reputation is better than a fat bank account.
Your death date tells more than your birth date.
You learn more at a funeral than at a feast—
After all, that's where we'll end up. We might discover something from it.
Crying is better than laughing.
It blotches the face but it scours the heart.
Sages invest themselves in hurt and grieving.
Fools waste their lives in fun and games.
You'll get more from the rebuke of a sage
Than from the song and dance of fools.
The giggles of fools are like the crackling of twigs
Under the cooking pot. And like smoke.
Brutality stupefies even the wise
And destroys the strongest heart.
Endings are better than beginnings.
Sticking to it is better than standing out.
Don't be quick to fly off the handle.
Anger boomerangs. You can spot a fool by the lumps on his head. . . .

On a good day, enjoy yourself;
On a bad day, examine your conscience.
God arranges for both kinds of days
So that we won't take anything for granted."
—ECCLESIASTES 7:1–9, 14 (MSG)

Dear Jesus,
Thank you for this day. Help me never to take Your gifts for granted.
Help me to . . .

Know That All We Have Are Gifts from Him

When you wake up in the morning, that is a gift. When you hang both legs over the side of the bed and drop your feet to start your day, that is a gift. When you open the fridge and find something to eat, that is a gift. When you pull out of the garage and head to work, that is a gift. When you have money for coffee, that is a gift. When you have family and friends, that is a gift. If you have someone to come home to, that is a gift. When you have the sun on your face, that is a gift. When the stars come out at night and light up the sky, that is a gift. When you believe that Jesus Christ died for your sins, giving you eternal life, that is a gift.

> "Every good and perfect gift is from above, coming down from the Father of the heavenly lights, who does not change like shifting shadows. He chose to give us birth through the word of truth, that we might be a kind of firstfruits of all he created."
> —JAMES 1:17–18

Thank you, Father. We know that all we have are gifts from You. Amen.

Dear Jesus,
Thank you for this day. Thank you for walking with me and for every good gift. I know they come from You! Help me to . . .

Find the Blessing

In my old life I used to love when everything was smooth sailing. I loved when there were no problems and nothing I could see coming down the path would interfere with my present happiness. But what I've discovered as I lean into the uncomfortable and challenging times and count it all joy is that this is when I learn to be more like Jesus.

Typically, there is something in the struggle—something that makes me think or question, something that challenges my way of thinking. And when I embrace that and open my heart to the teaching, I walk away with a different perspective and an understanding of the lesson.

How about you? Are you able to find the blessing, even in the challenging times? Are you able to be thankful for the gift of struggles and the lessons we learn when we go through them?

We all have tests in our life. But, ultimately, we are defined not by the things that will eventually come our way but by how we walk through those situations and come out the other side. Never forget that Jesus too walked a road that ended at a cross, but He overcame so that we might have everlasting life.

Dear Jesus,
Thank you for this day. Help me to find the blessings, even in the trials.
Help me to . . .

Use Your Gifts to Help Others

Have you ever seen the movie *Pay It Forward*? If you haven't, it's a definite must see that came out in 2000. It was based on the novel written by Catherine Ryan Hyde and recounts the 12-year-old life of Trevor Mckinney and his school project called "Pay it Forward" that went nationwide. To me, it's a wonderful example of how to be the hands and feet of Jesus. While living a life for Jesus can be more than helping just three people—which was the number in Trevor's project—ultimately it's giving of our time and our resources to help someone else. If you're praying to be open and are looking for ways you can use your gifts to help others, below is a short list of ideas that may help:

- Make a meal for someone who just had a baby or was hospitalized
- Offer free babysitting
- Send a card
- Pray with a friend
- Volunteer
- Have coffee and listen
- Help a stranger
- Pay for someone's meal
- Buy groceries for someone who is struggling
- Drive someone to an appointment

As you can see, it's not always about spending money but about being obedient and finding ways we can function as Jesus' hands and feet. I'm praying that you will be open today.

Dear Jesus,
I pray that You will use me today. Help me to be open to Your prompting to do Your will, for Your people and for Your glory. Amen.

Love in All You Do

L is the last letter in *THANKFUL*, and a wonderful way to segue into *loving in all that you do*. For the next few days we are going to camp here and focus on what it looks like to be the hands and feet of Jesus. While it may seem overwhelming wondering where to start, the best place is by asking Him for help. We start with prayer . . .

Lord,
I pray that You will use me today. Help me to be open to Your prompting to do
Your will, for Your people and for Your glory. Amen.

By saying this prayer each morning we keep ourselves and our eyes open to the people around us who are in need. When you stay open, God may place you in the path of someone who needs a smile, a kind word, or maybe even a warm cup of coffee. So have a beautiful day, be open, and see what God wants you to do.

Dear Jesus,
Thank you for this day. Help me to be open to Your promptings. Help
me to . . .

To Follow Jesus

So, how did it go the first day? Did anything special happen? Were you more aware of the people around you and their needs?

It's amazing that the smallest acts of kindness can sometimes bring the biggest smiles. And it's also amazing that most people aren't expecting it. Sometimes it feels as though our world is getting more and more negative. Which is another reason it's time for a change. Two thousand years ago Jesus was a man people wanted to be around, and not because he was going around buying them gifts. He was listening to them, loving them, talking with them, sharing a meal with them, and sharing God's Word.

I know that change doesn't always happen right away. But there is one decision we can make and keep making every day when we open our eyes—that we are going to follow Jesus. We live in a world full of things that will try to keep us from this, but if we keep our eyes on Him and keep making that decision our prize will be an eternity with Him!

Dear Jesus,
I pray that You will use me today. Help me to be open to Your prompting to do Your will, for Your people and for Your glory. Help me to . . .

His Hands and Feet

So, how did it go? Any life-changing stories? Have you been contemplating what it means to be Jesus' hands and feet? For me it was literally thinking about His hands and His feet; one of the last images I have of them was when He was here on earth, nailed to the cross, dying for my sin.

The same hands that healed and hugged and broke bread, and the same feet that walked mile after mile to teach, took the nails in my place. That is humbling and beautiful and reminds me that to follow Jesus and live the way He did comes at a price. It is not easy; there will be struggles, but it will be worth it. I know that someday I will see Him face to face, and for that I am THANKFUL! Amen.

Dear Jesus,

I pray that You will use me today and tomorrow and every day after that. Help me to be open to Your prompting to do Your will, for Your people and for Your glory. Help me to . . .

Blessed

Write down a list of the things you are thankful for. It can include anything or everything that comes to your mind.

"Give thanks to the LORD, for he is good;
his love endures forever."
—1 CHRONICLES 16:34

Dear Jesus,

Thank you for today. Thank you for Your many gifts. I am grateful and know that all these gifts pass through Your hands and come to me. Help me today to focus on these gifts and to remember how blessed I really am. Help me to . . .

A Way of Life

Mark Tidd of Webster, New York, describes an experience from his college days:

"An old man showed up at the back door of the house we were renting. Opening the door a few inches, we saw his eyes were glassy and his furrowed face glistened with silver stubble. He clutched a wicker basket holding a few unappealing vegetables. He bid us good morning and offered his produce for sale. We were uneasy enough that we made a quick purchase to alleviate both our pity and our fear.

To our chagrin, he returned the next week, introducing himself as Mr. Roth, the man who lived in the shack down the road. As our fears subsided, we got close enough to realize it wasn't alcohol but cataracts that marbleized his eyes. On subsequent visits, he would shuffle in, wearing two mismatched right shoes, and pull out a harmonica. With glazed eyes set on a future glory, he'd puff out old gospel tunes between conversations about vegetables and religion.

On one visit, he exclaimed, 'The Lord is so good! I came out of my shack this morning and found a bag full of shoes and clothing on my porch.'

'That's wonderful, Mr. Roth!' we said. 'We're happy for you.'

'You know what's even more wonderful?' he asked. 'Just yesterday I met some people that could really use them.'"

Thankfulness is not just a feeling—it's a way of life.

Dear Jesus,

Thank you for this day. Thank you for walking with me and for every good gift. I know they come from You! Thank you for . . .

The Big Picture

In Acts 4:32–37 Luke writes about the believers and how they did life together: "All the believers were one in heart and mind. No one claimed that any of their possessions was their own, but they shared everything they had. With great power the apostles continued to testify to the resurrection of the Lord Jesus. And God's grace was so powerfully at work in them all that there were no needy persons among them. For from time to time those who owned land or houses sold them, brought the money from the sales and put it at the apostles' feet, and it was distributed to anyone as he had need. Joseph, a Levite from Cyprus, whom the apostles called Barnabas (which means 'son of encouragement'), sold a field he owned and brought the money and put it at the apostles' feet."

Oh, to see the big picture and live together in harmony, peace, and gratitude. Today, let's spend less time thinking about what is ours and remember that everything we have comes from God. Is our sense of ownership justified, or does everything belong to Him?

Dear Jesus,

Thank you for today! Open my eyes to see and my ears to hear. Help me to see Your grand design. Help me to . . .

Thankful for the Painful Lessons

Today, write down the things that have been painful or challenging in your life, and why you are thankful they happened. Was there a lesson or a blessing that came out of the experience for which you are grateful?

"I will extol the LORD at all times;
> his praise will always be on my lips."
—PSALM 34:1

Painful or challenging event   Why you are thankful for it

Dear Jesus,

Thank you for today. Thank you for always walking with me. Thank you for the hard and challenging moments that grow and stretch me. Use these moments to make me more like You. Help me today to . . .

The Journey

After eleven years my job is changing again. In the beginning I started answering phones, putting together folders, doing odds and ends, and acting in the role of support staff. Over the years I proved myself, and my responsibilities increased. I was part of the sales team and had my real estate license. I managed the office and was involved in many integral decisions and meetings. I felt important and poured myself into my job.

But the day I heard God tell me it was time to tell my story, everything changed. I had no idea that over the next two years He would change my heart and fix my focus. When my first book was published, I knew that I would eventually give up my real estate license, and when the ministry started a new sales person was hired. I am now back to answering phones, putting together folders, doing odds and ends, and acting as support staff. Day by day responsibilities shift and move, until one day I know I will have nothing left to do and it will be time to leave.

There are moments when I want to grab at everything and take it all back. But in these moments God reminds me that I am on a new path. Corrie ten Boom once said, "Never be afraid to trust an unknown future to a known God!" While she was imprisoned for helping many Jews escape the Nazi Holocaust during World War II, her godly example shows us that God uses our journeys for His greater purpose. I am thankful that God is always more interested in the journey than the destination, and knowing what I know now I would travel the same road again, knowing it would bring me to Him. So, for now, I am thankful for each day, each folder I put together, each phone call I answer. I stay in the moment and wait for His call.

Dear Jesus,
I pray that You will use me today. Please help me have courage in the waiting and trust in Your plan. Help me to . . .

Looking Back

Looking back, I have sometimes wished that my parents never got a divorce. I have looked at other marriages that are going strong after twenty years and wondered, *Why couldn't that have been me?* I see the wasted years I spent drowning in my illness and thought I could've been a better mother, a better wife. I've counted all the money I've lost trying to fill an emptiness that could never be filled and have regretted a lot of the choices I made.

But when I look back, despite all of my mistakes, I look at all the blessings God so graciously gave me. I'm thankful for my children, for the jobs that allowed me to raise them, for the way Jesus walked with me even when I walked my own path. God also reminds me that no pain is ever wasted. When I look back, I realize that God used everything I encountered and endured to make me who I am today. For that, I wouldn't change a thing. I am grateful for His love, His patience, and that He never gave up on me.

Dear Jesus,

Thank you for today. Thank you for always walking with me. Thank you for the hard and challenging moments that grow and stretch me. Use these moments to make me more like You. Help me today to . . .

A Prayer for Today

Dear Lord,

Thank you for today. Help me to remember that my worth is not made up of the things I own, but that I am Yours, created in Your image. Thank you for the love of my family and friends. Thank you for what You're doing in my life. Thank you for the many blessings You give me each day, and that You never let go of my hand. You are a faithful God, and I praise You. I praise You even amidst the challenges of this world. I praise You even when things don't go my way. I praise You even when I can't see where this road leads. I praise You, Lord, and thank You, for You are all I need. Amen.

Dear Jesus,

Thank you for this day. Teach me to be thankful in all circumstances. Help me to . . .

The Light

Have you ever been afraid? Sometimes fear can paralyze us and we stay frozen in the moment, unable to move forward into the life God has prepared for us. Have you ever admitted what your fears are? In the past I've written mine down, which enabled me to see each one on the page and give them over to God. For that I am thankful. I'm thankful that bringing them out into the light allows God to work on each one and takes power away from the enemy and his darkness. Today, write down your fears and allow the Holy Spirit to help you bring them into the light . . .

> "When I am afraid, I put my trust in you.
>   In God, whose word I praise—
> in God I trust and am not afraid.
>   What can mere mortals do to me?"

—PSALM 56:3-4

Dear Jesus,
Thank you for this day. Thank you that I can lay before You my fears
and know that You will help me. Help me bring them out into the light.
Help me to overcome. Help me to . . .

Remain Faithful

How long will you stay thankful and wait on God to answer a prayer that you pray every day? For over a year I have prayed every day for healing for my mom. I have prayed for answers. I have prayed for her restoration. In that year, while we waited, I have seen her surrender, submit to the pain and to the list of questions she had for doctors and the questions she had for God. I've watched her choose joy, choose love, and choose to be obedient, day after day, month after month. Not my will, Lord, but Yours . . .

Now, over a year later, she is on medication to help with the pain. While she doesn't have answers and may never have them, she is awaiting her next adventure with God leading the way. He is answering her prayers and showering His faithful servant with love.

How long will you remain faithful and thankful, awaiting a word from God? I pray that I will wait forever, if that is how long I must wait, knowing that my God's timing is perfect and that He will give me the strength.

Dear Jesus,
Thank you for this day. Teach me to be thankful in all circumstances,
and give me patience in the waiting. Help me to . . .

Always Go Back

"Now on his way to Jerusalem, Jesus traveled along the border between Samaria and Galilee. As he was going into a village, ten men who had leprosy met him. They stood at a distance and called out in a loud voice, 'Jesus, Master, have pity on us!'

When he saw them, he said, 'Go, show yourselves to the priests.' And as they went, they were cleansed.

One of them, when he saw he was healed, came back, praising God in a loud voice. He threw himself at Jesus' feet and thanked him—and he was a Samaritan.

Jesus asked, 'Were not all ten cleansed? Where are the other nine? Has no one returned to give praise to God except this foreigner?' Then he said to him, 'Rise and go; your faith has made you well.'"

—LUKE 17:11-19

Forgive me, Lord, for the times I do not come back and say thank you! Today I thank You and praise You and love You. Thank you for my many gifts, for I know they come from You. Amen.

Dear Jesus,

Thank you for this day. Teach me to be thankful in all circumstances and remember to give You Your rightful praise. Help me to . . .

Choosing to Be Thankful

In a sermon at Immanuel Presbyterian Church in Los Angeles, Gary Wilburn said, "In 1636, amid the darkness of the Thirty Years' War, a German pastor, Martin Rinkart, is said to have buried five thousand of this parishioners in one year, an average of fifteen a day. His parish was ravaged by war, death, and economic disaster. In the heart of that darkness, with the cries of fear outside his window, he sat down and wrote this table grace for his children:

> 'Now thank we all our God
> With heart and hands and voices;
> Who wondrous things hath done,
> In whom his world rejoices.
> Who, from our mother's arms,
> Hath led us on our way
> With countless gifts of love
> And still is ours today.'

Here was a man who knew thanksgiving comes from the love of God, not from outward circumstances." Amen!

Dear Jesus,
Thank you for this day. Teach me to be thankful in all circumstances.
Help me to . . .

A Prayer for Today

Father God, Lord Jesus, Holy Spirit,

Thank you for my time with You this morning. Thank you for loving me and for giving me the gifts that You do in your most perfect timing. Help me to be fully present with You, to feel Your presence, to hear Your voice, to spend time with You.

Please forgive me for all the times I jump ahead, like a horse with no rein. Help me to wait on You, because that's when I feel affirmed in my direction forward.

I realize this morning, Lord, that I have everything I need to do Your will. I just have to believe. I have to have faith. I need to trust that You will equip me in the exact moment of my need.

Help me, Lord, not to be like Thomas. Help me, so that I don't feel a need to touch the holes in Your hands and see the mark in Your side. Let me have the kind of faith that can move mountains and step out into Your perfect will. Let that be my prayer today.

In Your most precious name I pray these things. Amen.

Dear Jesus,

Thank you for this day. Help me to . . .

When We Lean In

I've discovered as I lean into God and what He has for me a new feeling of uncomfortableness. There is not only the ebb and flow of happiness in my own life but also a feeling of empathy for others as they struggle. There is always someone dealing with illness. There is always someone dealing with financial heartache. There is always someone dealing with loss. There is always someone who still needs to know that Jesus loves them.

This uncomfortable feeling is new to me, and while I don't want to wish it away I can lean into it and know in the smallest way that this is how Jesus felt for all of us while He was here on earth. He moved in and out of people groups, absorbing their pain and loss and illness, and suffered with them.

This discomfort may also be feeling the weight, the heaviness, of picking up my cross and following Him. At times it's heavy and at other times awkward, but there is no place I would rather be than following Jesus to the ends of the earth . . . and into His sweet embrace in the next.

Dear Jesus,
Thank you for this day. Help me to lean into You and be mindful of the people around me who are hurting. Help me to . . .

Thankful for Today

Sometimes it's hard to be in the moment. I think that's because in this particular moment we may feel tired or distracted or be waiting for something. We are waiting for tomorrow because we expect it to be better or we have that special luncheon or plans with a friend. Tomorrow will be better because it's not supposed to rain, it's the weekend, it's payday, or this week will be over. Tomorrow has to be better than today because today was *really* tough.

If we move through life this way, anxious and waiting for tomorrow, we are going to miss all of our todays. We are going to miss the lessons we're supposed to learn, the people we're supposed to meet, and the gifts God wants to give us. If we miss today, we miss the gift of the rain, the joys of the weekdays, and the lessons in the hardships.

Jesus asked in Matthew 6:27, "'Can any one of you by worrying add a single hour to your life?'"

Today, be thankful for today! Rejoice in the fact that today is a gift; while tomorrow is unknown, it will come soon enough.

Dear Jesus,

Thank you for this day. Help me to be fully present today. Help me to . . .

The Season to Be Thankful

As we enter into this Thanksgiving season . . . are you overwhelmed? Sometimes we can be overwhelmed with the parties and the cooking and the travel. Maybe you're overwhelmed by the holiday itself and feel lonely because you're missing loved ones and family. Maybe you feel as though you have nothing to celebrate and can't wait for the day to be over. Whatever your situation, spend a few moments in your gratefulness and give God your feelings of loneliness, sadness, and stress. Take a few moments to write out what you're feeling right now . . .

> "And whatever you do, whether in word or deed, do it all in the name of the Lord Jesus, giving thanks to God the Father through him."
> —COLOSSIANS 3:17

Dear Jesus,
Thank you for this day. Help me to . . .

One Thing

If I had to be thankful for just one thing, I would choose what Jesus did for me on the cross.

> "He was pierced for our transgressions,
>   he was crushed for our iniquities;
> the punishment that brought us peace was on him,
>   and by his wounds we are healed."
> —ISAIAH 53:5

What He did changed my whole life, and because of His sacrifice I have the promise of eternity with Him.

> "For it is by grace you have been saved, through faith—and this is not from yourselves, it is the gift of God—not by works, so that no one can boast. For we are God's handiwork, created in Christ Jesus to do good works, which God prepared in advance for us to do."
> —EPHESIANS 2:8-10

Thank you, Lord, for the gift of salvation and what You did on the cross! I am forever grateful!

Below, write down the one thing you are most thankful for.

Dear Jesus,

Thank you for today. Thank you for Your many gifts. I am grateful and know that all these gifts pass through Your hands to come to me. Help me today to focus on these gifts and to remember how blessed I really am. Help me to . . .

Black Friday

D o you find it ironic that the day after we spend the day being thankful for all the things we have, we celebrate a day called Black Friday when we go out and buy more stuff? And it seems as of late that the pace and pressure surrounding these sales have intensified. Now you can go out and shop right after you're done with your meal.

I'm not against a good deal, but don't get caught up in the cycle of this world and what's selling in commercials. It's not a better way of life. It's not what you need. It won't take away your problems or make you whole. Only Jesus can do that.

> "Do not store up for yourselves treasures on earth, where moths and vermin destroy, and where thieves break in and steal. But store up for yourselves treasures in heaven, where moths and vermin do not destroy, and where thieves do not break in and steal. For where your treasure is, there your heart will be also."
> —MATTHEW 6:19-21

Dear Jesus,
Thank you for today. Help me to focus on what's truly important in this life. Set me apart and help me to live in this world, but not be of this world. Help me to . . .

Always Give Thanks to God

I hope you found this month valuable and have developed new ways to look at being thankful. Whatever season you are in right now, whether it's one filled with blessings or you're searching to find them, may you experience the peace of Christ and "let the message of Christ dwell among you richly as you teach and admonish one another with all wisdom through psalms, hymns, and songs from the Spirit, singing to God with gratitude in your hearts. And whatever you do, whether in word or deed, do it all in the name of the Lord Jesus, giving thanks to God the Father through him" (Colossians 3:16–17).

Dear Jesus,
Thank you for this day. Thank you for everything that I have, for I know it comes from You. Help me to have a thankful heart. Help me to . . .

December

CHRISTMAS CHANGES EVERYTHING

"For to us a child is born,
to us a son is given, and the
government will be on his shoulders.
And he will be called Wonderful
Counselor, Mighty God,
Everlasting Father, Price of Peace."

–ISAIAH 9:6

Always Winter, Never Christmas

In C. S. Lewis's book *The Lion, the Witch and the Wardrobe*, the White Witch has cast her spell on Narnia, decreeing that it must always be winter but never Christmas. At one time in my own life, I felt as though I were standing in the middle of a snowstorm and couldn't see. I was waiting for the promise you feel when you open your eyes and it is Christmas morning. But all I felt was the snow on my face and the fear that I was walking in the wrong direction, with no idea how to get home.

Even though this season felt as though it would never end, eventually the sun did show itself again and winter turned to spring. In the morning I could hear birds chirping, and before long flowers pushed their way to the surface and buds appeared on the trees. It was a reminder that our difficult seasons don't last forever. They are seasons, and when we come through to the other side the beauty we see is that much more beautiful and our senses that much more intensified. God does not promise that this life will be easy but that He will walk with us and never forsake us. And this promise came to fruition when He sent His Son to be born one Christmas morning. Jesus changed everything, my friends, and all this month we are going to look at why and how.

Dear Jesus,

Thank you for this day. Thank you for leaving the comfort of heaven and wanting to walk with us here on earth. Thank you for loving me that much. Help me to fully understand what You did for me and how it changed everything. Help me to . . .

In the Beginning

In the beginning . . .

Do you think He knew? I mean in the beginning, when God was breathing life into the world and forming Adam and Eve, did He know that He would someday need to send His Son to walk among us and die for our sins? He's God, and He knows everything, so He would have to have known. And yet He was willing to do it anyway—to create everything for us, knowing full well that we would turn our faces away from Him, destroy His creation, and crucify His Son. What kind of love is that?

I would say it's an amazing kind of love . . .

"In the beginning, Lord, you laid the foundations of the earth,
    and the heavens are the work of your hands."
—HEBREWS 1:10

Dear Jesus,

Thank you for today. Thank you for loving us despite our sin. Thank you for sending Your Son. Help me to . . .

The Perfect Holiday

There was a time in my life when everything had to be perfect at Christmas. I needed our house to shine with the outdoor lights and to enjoy the real tree experience, my Christmas cards had to say just the right thing, and my cookies needed to be perfect. But little did I know that as exhausting as it was to create this perfect holiday, none of these things were needed to do so. The gift wasn't in the lights, the tree, the cards, or the cookies. The gift wasn't what I could do, but what God had already done for me. Sending His Son, Jesus, changed everything, and when I realized that . . . it even changed me.

I encourage you to be mindful of the Christmas you create this year. If your usual festivities make you lose sight of the real reason you're celebrating, then give those over to God. Find a way to make Jesus the reason for this season.

"For God so loved the world that he gave his one and only Son, that whoever believes in him shall not perish but have eternal life."
—JOHN 3:16

Dear Jesus,
Thank you for this day. Help me to remember that this season is about You and the gift You are. Help me to . . .

The Loneliest Time of Year

Christmas can be a lonely time, a time when we're missing those people in our lives who are far away or have chosen to leave us. It can also be a time when you look back in your life to Christmases long ago, spent with parents and grandparents, brothers and sisters, aunts and uncles, some of whom are now gone. Maybe all have gone, and this year you are celebrating alone. But remember, you are never alone. You are loved by a Father who sent His Son for you. "Be strong and courageous. Do not be afraid; do not be discouraged, for the LORD your God will be with you wherever you go" (Joshua 1:9).

This year, if the loneliness comes, reach out to a neighbor or a friend. Volunteer at a soup kitchen or bring a meal to a family in need. Surprise a stranger with a gift. When we give to others and share our hearts, loneliness flees and we make new memories and new friends and enlarge our current family . . . the family of God.

> "Do you not know?
>   Have you not heard?
> The LORD is the everlasting God,
>   the Creator of the ends of the earth.
> He will not grow tired or weary,
>   and his understanding no one can fathom.
> He gives strength to the weary
>   and increases the power of the weak."
> —ISAIAH 40:28–29

Dear Jesus,

Thank you for this day. Thank you that I can bring You my burdens and sorrows. I'm lonely today. I'm missing . . . Help me in my loneliness. Help me to . . .

Take What You Need

Imagine an 8 ½ x 11" sign in a grocery store, stuck to the community bulletin board advertising a babysitting service or a cleaning lady. But instead of their service being advertised, the sign reads *Take What You Need*, and instead of their phone number dangling from the bottom to pull off, there are the pull-off words *love, hope, faith, healing, peace,* and *freedom.* As you stand there, ready to grab your shopping cart, which word would you grab? Which word do you desperately need right now? Do you know that they are *all* available to you? That instead of standing there deciding on one, you can take the entire paper and put it in your cart?

I don't think we realize sometimes that this is why Jesus came. He came to do the will of His Father. He came to save us from sin. He came to bring light into this dark world. He came to bring the gospel. He came to seek the lost and heal the sick. He came to die for our sins so that we could have everlasting life. And in doing all of these things, He gave us love, hope, faith, healing, peace, and freedom in Christ.

This season, take what you need. It's all a gift, bought for you by the one true Savior, Jesus Christ. And it's free for the taking . . .

Dear Jesus,

Thank you for this day. Today, I choose You. I'm putting the entire offer in my cart because I need You, Lord. Help me to . . .

Love

It's not superficial. It's not temporary. It doesn't come with conditions or timelines or empty promises. It's not because of how you look or where you were born, or where you went to school. It doesn't care how much money you have, or how little, whether you have a home or even if you're living out of your car. It doesn't look at your past or the mistakes that you've made or consider whether you'll make more.

It just is. It's just there. It's ready for you to reach out and grab it. It's ready for you hold it close to your heart and feel that it's alive. It's ready for you to take it in and have it wash over you, purifying every cell. It will change the way you think about yourself and others. It will open your eyes and your ears to the truth, and you will crave His living Word.

It's His love. The same love that healed the lame, freed the slave, raised the dead, fed the hungry, calmed the sea, and died for you and me. Can't you feel it? Can't you see it? All you have to do is reach out and grab it. It's His love. And He's waiting for you . . .

Dear Jesus,
Thank you for this day. Thank you for loving me! Help me to feel Your love wash over me. Help me to . . .

Hope

Do you have hope? Not the kind where you hope you'll get a raise or hope your favorite team will win. The kind of hope I'm talking about is believing with everything you are that God is on your side. It's believing that God created you, loves you, and has a plan for your life. Sometimes believing this is challenging because this life is filled with struggle.

But when we hope in the Lord and trust in His plan, we will have joy in the mourning and the strength to travel whatever road we're on in spite of whatever is against us. Paul writes in Romans 8:31–32, "What, then, shall we say in response to these things? If God is for us, who can be against us? He who did not spare his own Son, but gave him up for us all—how will he not also, along with him, graciously give us all things?"

This Christmas, hope in Jesus. Believe that He is on your side and loves you with an everlasting love!

Dear Jesus,

Thank you for this day. Open my ears to hear and my heart to understand whatever You want to say. Thank you that You came to give us hope and life and a new name. Let me remember that I am Your child and that You came to earth for me. Help me to . . .

Faith

I have found that it is in the most difficult situations that we want to have faith. We cry out to God, some of us for the first time, in the hallways of the hospital, or alongside the road after an accident. We search for Him in the smoke-filled rooms of a house engulfed in flames, or standing beside the grave of someone we love. I've even seen the criminal cry out to God while stuck in a store he tried to rob but could find no way out of. Over and over he cried His name, having exhausted all other means and giving in to his fate.

When I see this time and time again, it makes me wonder how people can believe there is no God or that they can live without Him—when eventually we all cry out to Him. It's easy not to feel a need for Him when life is going smoothly and everything is going our way. Then the faith we have is in ourselves. But when things start to spin out of control, we see that control is really an illusion and we instinctively cry out to our Creator.

What if, starting this Christmas season, we were to reach for God, not only in the hard times but all the time? What if we were to start believing that we were created for a purpose, that God loves us, and that He sent His Son to give us the gift of everlasting life? All we have to do is reach out our hand and take it. All we have to do is trust in the promises of His Word and open the door to our hearts. All we have to do is have faith as tiny as a mustard seed, and we can move mountains. Do you believe? Do you have faith?

Dear Jesus,
Thank you for this day. Today, help me to grow in my faith. Help me to . . .

Healing

I know that Jesus heals. I know beyond the accounts I read in the Bible that happened over two thousand years ago. He heals today. I know, because He healed me. I was diagnosed with bipolar disorder in 1996, and my life tragically spun out of control. For four years I struggled with the manic/depressive swings and did what I wanted, not caring what God thought. One morning I stood in the kitchen and felt the full weight of all of my choices, and with nowhere else to turn I turned back to God. I surrendered my life and said I would do whatever He would ask—I just couldn't do this life anymore on my own.

He could've healed me right then. He could've taken away the illness and supernaturally fixed everything in one wave of His hand. But what would that have taught me? How would I have learned to live in this world?

He waited until 2013. He waited until I had walked a very challenging and difficult path for 13 years, drawing closer and closer to Him and learning the lessons He put before me. When the healing came, Jesus not only took the mental illness but healed every other aspect in my life, from my earliest memory, and made me whole again—back to His original design.

If, today, you are waiting for healing, ask God what it is that He wants you to learn. Jesus came not only to bring healing but to restore our lives and give us everlasting life. His viewpoint is much higher than ours, and He knows what we need. May it be in His timing and for His glory. Amen.

Dear Jesus,

Thank you for this day. I pray for healing, Lord, not only in body but in mind and spirit. Make me more like You. Help me to . . .

Peace

Prince of Peace. Do you have peace in your life? If not, I encourage you to invite Jesus into your unrest. He can calm the greatest storm, quiet the raging waters, whisper the sweetest words to bring peace to your spirit. Relax in Him today. Ask Jesus to give you this kind of peace: "and the peace of God, which transcends all understanding, will guard your hearts and your minds in Christ Jesus" (Philippians 4:7).

> "For to us a child is born,
>   to us a son is given,
> and the government will be on his shoulders.
>   And he will be called
> Wonderful Counselor, Mighty God,
>   Everlasting Father, Prince of Peace."
> —ISAIAH 9:6

Dear Jesus,
Thank you for this day. Today, I ask for Your peace. Please let me feel it like a warm blanket wrapped around me, quieting my heart. Help me to . . .

Freedom

What does freedom feel like and sound like to you? Is it the long-awaited breaking of chains? Is it the crash when they hit the floor and the instantaneous relief in your wrists and arms? Is it the sound of the key entering the lock; the clicking of the prison door; or the "clang, clang, clang, clang" as the door rolls open and you're freed to walk through?

You can be free—free from the chains of sin, free from the bondage of lies, free from the prison that the enemy tries to keep you in. Today, in Jesus' name, claim your freedom and rebuke the enemy. We are all free, free indeed!

> "You, my brothers and sisters, were called to be free. But do not use your freedom to indulge the flesh; rather, serve one another humbly in love. For the entire law is fulfilled in keeping this one command: 'Love your neighbor as yourself.'"
> —GALATIANS 5:13–14

Dear Jesus,
Thank you for this day. Help me today to feel the chains break and the door open up. Help me to recognize the lies of the enemy and to know that I was designed to be free. Help me to use my freedom to love others. Help me to . . .

Never Forget

Sometimes I forget how big God is. I forget that He does hear my prayers. I forget that He has a plan for my life. I forget that He knows everything about me . . . because He created me. And in spite of my sin, He loves me anyway. I forget that He made the heavens and the earth and is big enough to orchestrate everything that happened in the Bible . . . and everything that happens now.

Sometimes I forget momentarily, but when that second is over the truth comes rushing back in. I'm overwhelmed by the colors of the sky, the contours of the land, and the diversity of His creation. I'm awestruck that He would leave heaven and come to earth as a man so He could walk among us and we could know Him better.

> *You, who have spared me*
> *no life lesson.*
> *splurging on every sunrise.*
> *splashing colors across*
> *your horizon at day's end.*
> *warming days,*
> *cooling nights.*
> *sending love in every*
> *form you've made.*
> *sacrificing your only Son.*
> *spilling blood*
> *for every sin*
> *committed by me.*
>
> AMMIE BOUWMAN

Dear Jesus,

Thank you for today. Help me to never forget how big You are. Help me to . . .

The Wait Is Over

As we move through December, it's hard to contain our excitement. We sometimes use Advent calendars to count off the days before we celebrate Jesus' birth. But can you imagine that instead of waiting days we would have had to wait one thousand years? The first Christmas had been prophesied for hundreds of years, as we read in Isaiah 7:14: "Therefore the Lord himself will give you a sign: The virgin will conceive and give birth to a son, and will call him Immanuel." Eight decades later the angel Gabriel came to Mary and let her know she would give birth to a son and that His name would be Jesus.

The waiting is over, my friends! We can rejoice with all the saints that He is coming soon. Praise God.

Dear Jesus,

Thank you for today. Thank you that we no longer have to wait but can celebrate that You were born, walked this earth, and died for our sins. Thank you that Christmas has changed everything! Help me today to be present in this moment and reflect on what that means for my life. Help me today to . . .

A Season of Change

The summer of my birth in Grand Rapids, Michigan, was in the year that President Nixon lowered the voting age to eighteen, the first artificial gene was synthesized, and "Everything Is Beautiful" by Ray Stevens hit number one. The United States also celebrated its first Earth Day in 1970, and the United States Environmental Protection Agency was established. And on August 26 the Women's Strike for Equality was a nationwide demonstration on Fifth Avenue in New York City. It was held on the fiftieth anniversary of women being granted the right to vote.

Among all of these life-changing events, I was born—seven pounds eleven ounces, twenty-one inches long. My mother said my screams rang down the hallway of the hospital: my desire to be heard starting before I was fully out into the world.

They would give me the name Ammie, which means "beloved," and I would start my journey in this world, moving away from the "idealism and alienation, rebellion and backlash," as Kenneth T. Walsh describes the previous decade, toward microwave ovens, mood rings, newer thinking, and revolutionary ideas.

And, much as Jesus changed everything for Mary, everything changed for my 16-year-old mother. A child herself, she would need to learn to navigate these new waters and realize that nothing would ever be the same. If you are in a season of change, walking in unfamiliar territory and feeling afraid and alone, trust that the Lord is walking next to you and that He'll never let go of your hand.

Dear Jesus,

Thank you for today. Thank you that although change is hard You promise to walk with us and never leave us. Thank you that You are the one constant in an ever-changing world. Help me today to . . .

Ask, and You Shall Recieve

I t was November 16, 2004. I was helping my mom move to Santa Fe, New Mexico. We were settled in our motel for the night, and our goal for the next day was to find her a place to live. I knew she was nervous. She asked the front desk for a newspaper and started looking, her demeanor changing. Even though I hadn't completely understood her leaving, I tried to be positive about every aspect of the trip. So I grabbed part of the paper and in my most confident voice started rattling off some choices. Before long I think she felt better, because she knew she wasn't alone and eventually would find something.

She asked me if I wouldn't mind doing something with her—if we could pray together about her finding a place and leaving it in God's hands. So that's what we did. A very humbling thing to be on your knees in a hotel room, 1,250 miles from home, asking God to help you. And to kneel with your mother, whom you have to leave in five short days, whether she has a home or not, is a very surreal experience. But we serve a God who is bigger than our experiences, bigger than our fears, bigger than our situations. He knew exactly what we needed and provided the most perfect place for her, the very next day.

Don't be afraid to pray wherever you are or whatever you need. And never forget that Jesus with us changes everything. Amen!

Dear Jesus,
Thank you for today. Help me to remember why I'm celebrating You.
Help me to . . .

A Day of Healing

Another day I will never forget is March 22, 2013. I arrived at 10:00 a.m. for a day of healing and didn't leave until after 8:00 p.m. It had taken all day, but the bitterness, resentment, fear, shame, guilt, and confusion I had been carrying around all those years was gone. I had walked in looking like a woman who had been on a yearlong trip, with all my suitcases and baggage—and walked out carrying only my purse.

But once God healed me and my foundation was established, He needed to speak truth into all the areas of my life that had been broken, so I would never pick up those suitcases of lies again. I needed to start with the lie that had done the most damage, so I started at the beginning, 43 years earlier, on that warm day in June. It wasn't by accident that I had entered this world. Even though my parents were young and without a plan, God had a plan, and it included me. I would no longer believe that I was anything but chosen and loved by God. I would believe that I was His beloved.

Today, ask Jesus to speak truth into any lies you are believing. Remember, you are chosen and loved.

Dear Jesus,
Thank you for this day. Guard me with Your angels and protect me from the enemy. Speak truth into all areas of my life. Help me to . . .

He Is My Everything

After God spoke truth into my life, false guilt was my next lesson. I had grieved the loss of my first marriage and believed that it was all my fault. But marriage is made up of two people, both choosing to make the marriage work or let it fail. I would need to take responsibility for the mistakes I had made, ask forgiveness, and let it go. I would always love my first husband and be thankful for the time we had spent together and for the two beautiful children we had. But it was time to look forward and let go of the guilt.

God also showed me the truth about my second marriage and how it wasn't going to fix everything in my life. The companionship and security for which I longed would only be found in Jesus Christ. He wanted to be my everything.

Dear Jesus,

Thank you for today. Thank you for loving me and wanting to be my everything. Help me to believe that. Help me to . . .

A Star

I've never followed a star like the wise men, but I've prayed to see one, and God answered my prayer. "God, since you are the Creator of the universe, I need a sign from heaven that I'm healed. I need to see a shooting star." And one morning on my way to work, the first day going without my medication after five days of half my pills, I saw my star, and that was all the confirmation I needed. I had been set free!

I fully embraced the new me, even though she was foreign and strange. The view before me was of a shimmering sea: different from the earth I had climbed up from and the many hills I had wandered through during my illness. I was now living on the waves, and it took time to adjust to the normal flow of emotion and the evenness I felt. But those who knew me best saw my change. God had completely healed me of my bipolar disorder, and I would never again doubt His miraculous power or His ability to heal again.

> "In all these things we are more than conquerors through him who loved us. For I am convinced that neither death nor life, neither angels nor demons, neither the present nor the future, nor any powers, neither height nor depth, nor anything else in all creation, will be able to separate us from the love of God that is in Christ Jesus our Lord."
> —ROMANS 8:37–39

Dear Jesus,
Thank you for today. Help me to live on the waves and trust You. Help me to . . .

A Reason for Everything

I mentioned in the introduction that it was at the top of the Makhtesh Ramon that I heard God tell me it was time to tell my story. But the question didn't hit me until months after I came home from Israel: *Why did He tell me there?* God never does anything by chance; there is always a reason for everything. The pieces started coming together until this is what I saw. He brought me to the world's largest *makhtesh*, not formed by an impact but by tectonic forces. The explanation that tectonic forces are rocks under stress that are subjected to a force at depth had at first been literally over my head, but now I understood that *I* too was being remade by the ultimate force: God.

Whatever you're going through right now, trust in the Lord. He has a perfect plan. You may not see it now, but when you look back every piece will fall into place. Trust as He takes the broken pieces of your life and creates something beautiful!

Dear Jesus,

Thank you for today. Thank you that You never do anything by chance. Help me to trust You as You take my broken pieces and make something beautiful of them. Help me to . . .

Obedience Without Understanding

Do you know the story of Mary, the mother of Jesus? According to ancient Jewish custom she was probably around 12 years old when she was betrothed to Joseph. It's hard for me to understand what that would look like because when my daughter was 12 she was learning how to play soccer and the complexities of decimals and fractions. She would not have understood the angel of the Lord appearing to her, being overshadowed by the Holy Spirit, and conceiving in her the Son of God.

> "This is how the birth of Jesus the Messiah came about: His mother Mary was pledged to be married to Joseph, but before they came together, she was found to be pregnant through the Holy Spirit. Because Joseph her husband was faithful to the law, and yet did not want to expose her to public disgrace, he had in mind to divorce her quietly.
>
> But after he had considered this, an angel of the Lord appeared to him in a dream and said, 'Joseph, son of David, do not be afraid to take Mary home as your wife, because what is conceived in her is from the Holy Spirit. She will give birth to a son, and you are to give him the name Jesus, because he will save his people from their sins.'"
> —MATTHEW 1:18-21

Has God ever asked you to do something that you didn't understand? Were you obedient? Praying that today you will ask for God's strength to equip you for whatever He would ask of you.

Dear Jesus,

Thank you for today. Thank you for Mary. Thank you for her innocent, obedient spirit and her faithfulness to do whatever You asked of her. Help me to be obedient. Help me to . . . . . .

Mary's Song

After Mary had heard from the angel Gabriel that she would be with child, she went and stayed with her relative Elizabeth, who was also going to have a baby, another miracle as she was considered barren and beyond childbearing years.

When Mary arrived and the two women greeted each other, the baby in Elizabeth's womb leapt for joy. She would give birth to John the Baptist, and he would prepare the way for Jesus.

While staying with Elizabeth, Mary wrote these words: "'My soul glorifies the Lord and my spirit rejoices in God my Savior, for he has been mindful of the humble state of his servant. From now on all generations will call me blessed, for the Mighty One has done great things for me—holy is his name. His mercy extends to those who fear him, from generation to generation. He has performed mighty deeds with his arm; he has scattered those who are proud in their inmost thoughts. He has brought down rulers from their thrones but has lifted up the humble. He has filled the hungry with good things but has sent the rich away empty. He has helped his servant Israel, remembering to be merciful to Abraham and his descendants forever, just as he preomised our ancestors'" (Luke 1:46–55).

Dear Jesus,

Thank you for today. Thank you for Your own mother, Mary. Thank you for her innocent, obedient spirit and her faithfulness to do whatever Your Father asked of her. Help me to be obedient. Help me to . . .

In All Things God Works for Good

When you read Matthew1:1–16, you'll see a stunning example of how God weaves lives together for His glory. The writer, Matthew, is very intentional in writing out Jesus' genealogy, listing name after name, representing story after story of how broken people can be used by God. Each one had made mistakes, each one had sinned and fallen short, but even then God was restoring them to show that "in all things God works for the good of those who love him, who have been called according to his purpose" (Romans 8:28).

There were 14 generations in all from Abraham to David, 14 from David to the exile to Babylon, and 14 from the exile to Jesus. Perfection.

Today, look back and see the restoration in your past. Look and see how God is doing something new. And if you can't see it in your past, maybe He is just getting started with you.

Dear Jesus,

Thank you for today. Show me what You are doing in my life. Help me to see Your amazing transformations. If not in my past, then begin Your new work in my life right now. Help me to . . .

What Does Christmas Mean to You?

What does Christmas mean to you? Is it more than the tree and the cookies and the Christmas cards? Is it more than the gifts and the parties? What has Jesus done in your life that has changed everything? Take a few moments and think about all the things Jesus has done, and what this Christmas means to you . . .

Dear Jesus,
Thank you for today. Thank you for all the things You have done for me and continue to do. Help me to focus on what Christmas really means, and not on what the world tells me it is. Help me to spend these next days celebrating You. Help me to . . .

Chistmas Eve

A re you ready? You can almost hear how still the world is in anticipation. It's not the magic of Christmas that we're told about in books and movies that is creating this excitement we feel. It's our spirit inside us proclaiming the great news of the coming Messiah.

> "He will be great and will be called the Son of the Most High. The Lord God will give him the throne of his father David, and he will reign over Jacob's descendants forever; his kingdom will never end."
> —LUKE 1:32–33

So quiet your mind. Put aside the busyness you may be experiencing and relish the fact that tomorrow everything will change.

Dear Jesus,
Thank you for today. Help me to quiet my mind and focus on You. Help me to . . .

Merry Christmas

Merry Christmas, my friend! Wishing you a blessed day and the greatest gift ever given—Jesus Christ!

"And there were shepherds living out in the fields nearby, keeping watch over their flocks at night. An angel of the Lord appeared to them, and the glory of the Lord shone around them, and they were terrified. But the angel said to them, 'Do not be afraid. I bring you good news that will cause great joy for all the people. Today in the town of David a Savior has been born to you; he is the Messiah, the Lord. This will be a sign to you: You will find a baby wrapped in cloths and lying in a manger.'

Suddenly a great company of the heavenly host appeared with the angel, praising God and saying,

'Glory to God in the highest heaven,
and on earth peace to men on whom his favor rests.'"
—LUKE 2:8–14

Dear Jesus,
Thank you for today. Thank you for the many gifts You give us, but mostly thank you for You! I give You all the praise and glory for . . .

The Wise Men

The Magi would have known the writings of the prophet Daniel, which gives a timeline for His birth. They followed the constellations and watched the stars align. They came bearing gifts: gold, frankincense, and myrrh. But most of all they were obedient—which made them truly wise men!

"After Jesus was born in Bethlehem in Judea, during the time of King Herod, Magi from the east came to Jerusalem and asked, 'Where is the one who has been born king of the Jews? We saw his star when it rose and have come to worship him.'

When King Herod heard this he was disturbed, and all Jerusalem with him. . . .

Then Herod called the Magi secretly and found out from them the exact time the star had appeared. He sent them to Bethlehem and said, 'Go and search carefully for the child. As soon as you find him, report to me, so that I too may go worship him.'

After they had heard the king, the went on their way, and the star they had seen when it rose went ahead of them until it stopped over the place where the child was. When the saw the star, they were overjoyed. On coming to the house, they saw the child with his mother Mary, and they bowed down and worshiped him. Then they opened their treasures and presented him with gifts of gold, frankincense and myrrh. And having been warned in a dream not to go back to Herod, they returned to their country by another route."

—MATTHEW 2:1-3, 7-12

Dear Jesus,

Thank you for today. Thank you for the wise men and that they were obedient to You. Help me to follow You wherever You lead. Help me . . .

The Journey

When I look back at my life and what I've gone through, I realize I wouldn't change a thing. Sure, I have regret. I've made plenty of mistakes, traveled down the wrong roads, made poor choices, and hurt the people around me. But if I hadn't done those things, walking through each lesson that God showed me, I wouldn't be who I am today. I wouldn't have the appreciation I have for the peaceful seasons, and the seasons when I have plenty, because I've been through the storm and have lived without. We're all on different journeys, but with one destination in view: heaven. This life is only a blip on the radar compared to the eternity we will have with Jesus.

What you need to focus on today is whether you are willing to look at your life and see where you're going. Are you moving forward with Jesus toward a life of eternity? Or are you traveling down the wrong road, maybe living in the past and not sure how to get back? You can always stop and turn around and cry out to Him. Nothing you have done will ever change His mind . . . He will always love you. He came for you, over two thousand years ago, to walk this earth and die on a cross on your behalf. If it had only been you . . . He still would've come.

Dear Jesus,

Thank you for this day. Thank you for loving me in spite of the choices I've made and the path that I've been on. Help me get back to You. Help me to . . .

A Prayer for Today

Lord,

I so look forward to this time with You, reflecting on my life and what I've learned. Thank you for today. Thank you that Christmas changes everything. I give to You my worries, my past, my future. Help me to trust in You. Thank you that You have given me a better way of life. I am the way I am today only because of Your grace and mercy. Please take from me any shred of my past and make me free. I give it to You, Lord, to cast into the deepest part of the farthest ocean, never to appear again. Even when it's asked about, I will be calm. You can have it all, Lord. I hold nothing back and give it all to You. In Jesus' precious name, Amen.

Dear Jesus,

Thank you for this day. Thank you for loving me enough to come to earth and show me how to live like You. Help me to let go of my past and give You my future. Help me to . . .

Heaven on Earth

How do we die to self and become more like Christ—more like the way He designed us to be? We read about Him in His Word. We spend time with Him each day, opening our hearts and minds and learning to listen for His voice. We spend a year as we've just done wanting to grow closer to Him and become more like Him.

It's possible, my friends. It's possible to spend time with someone day after day and learn how to be like them. How do I know this? A prime example is living with my mom this last year. I wasn't even trying to be like her, and now I find myself washing out Ziploc bags and doing things I've never done before. She wasn't trying to teach me these things, wasn't pushing me to learn something new. She was just living her life, and that's what Jesus does when He comes alongside someone. He loves on them. That's who He is.

And that is how we can show love to other people. We act like Christ, day in and day out doing our normal things. And before long people will start to pick up on what we're doing and start acting as we act. One day we'll wake up and there's not one person acting like Christ, not five people acting like Christ, not a thousand-people acting like Christ, . . . but the entire world acting like Christ, loving each other and showing kindness to one another. And *that*, my friends, will be heaven on earth . . .

Dear Jesus,

Thank you for this day. Thank you for this past year. Help me to continue to grow in You, act like You, and love others like You. Let my life be an example of Your love. Help me to . . .

Are You Ready?

Are you ready to surrender? Are you ready to fall into His arms and let go? Are you ready to let go of who you were, where you've been, and where you're going? Don't you think it's time? If today is the day, say this prayer:

> *I thank You, Lord, for the life You've given me.*
> *The joy that I've known I have not deserved.*
> *You did not leave my side, ever.*
> *And when You could've walked away,*
> *You picked me up again and again.*
> *I do now what You have wanted for so long,*
> *and I do it with the world as my witness;*
> *I surrender myself to You, God Almighty.*
> *Whatever happens from here, Your will be done.*

Dear Jesus,
Thank you for this day. Help me today feel the chains break and the doors open wide. Help me to surrender my life to You. Help me to . . .

Your Glorious Future

It's New Year's Eve. We've spent the last year counting it all joy, leaving Egypt for the promised land, walking toward the cross, letting go, looking at our authentic selves, discovering a manual for living, remembering that the greatest of these is love, saying our Hallelujahs in the hard times, conversing with God, discovering all the reasons we're thankful, and knowing that Christmas changes everything.

Thank you for taking this journey. Thank you for your willingness to walk with me and dig deeper. I pray that you've discovered not only more about God but more about yourself. I pray that you will choose to stay on this path toward truth and that, when the road gets dark, you'll remember that Jesus is holding your hand. I pray that you will always know that you are here for a reason, created by God for His purpose and for His glory. When you surrender your life, let go of the past and move forward in faith, you are walking toward your glorious future . . . and it is beautiful!

But even more, I pray that, like me, you will step out into the waters of life and realize it is better to be like Peter and be out of the boat walking toward Jesus than safe on the shore. Even if that means we will live on the waves and at times be in over our head . . .

God Bless! Go in Peace and love!
Until we meet again,
Ammie Bouwman